ROYCE AND HOCKING — AMERICAN IDEALISTS

ROYCE AND HOCKING
AMERICAN IDEALISTS

An Introduction to Their Philosophy, With Selected Letters

By

DANIEL SOMMER ROBINSON, PhD., Litt.D.

Director Emeritus, School of Philosophy,
University of Southern California

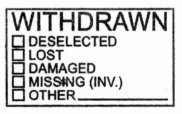

THE CHRISTOPHER PUBLISHING HOUSE
BOSTON, U. S. A.

To the memory

of

Josiah Royce

and

William Ernest Hocking

in

appreciation of the inspiration

received from

their teachings and their writings

TABLE OF CONTENTS

FOREWORD

Josiah Royce and William Ernest Hocking were the founders and creators of a unique and distinctly American school of idealistic philosophy. Throughout the present volume, I refer to this school as the Royce-Hocking type of American idealism. The combined publications of these two philosophers extend over a period of more than ninety years, and in its entirety constitutes a most impressive and significant body of philosophical literature. A complete exposition and critical examination of all their writings would, of course, require volumes. Therefore, my principal objectives are to provide a general introduction to their thought, to clarify its chief characteristics, and to induce readers to study seriously their chief works.

During the past twenty years I have had occasion to write several essays on various aspects of the Royce-Hocking type of American metaphysical idealism. During this time, I have maintained personal contacts with Hocking and with Stephen Royce, son of Josiah Royce. The essays are scattered throughout various books and journals, some being relatively inaccessible, and most of the correspondence has never been published. Consequently, for the benefit of future students and scholars, I am assembling in the present volume all of these relevant essays, including one not previously published, and also the pertinent correspondence. The material is arranged in three parts. Part One: *Essays on the Philosophy of Josiah Royce;* Part Two: *Essays on the Philosophy of William Ernest Hocking;* and Part Three: *Selected Letters.*

Among those Harvard University doctoral graduates who took advanced courses under both of these inspiring teachers, I am possibly the only living exponent of the Royce-Hocking type of metaphysical idealism. Hocking, himself, received graduate instruction from Royce at Harvard University. He was serving as a member of the Department of Philosophy at Yale University when the Yale Press published his *magnum opus, The Meaning of God in Human Experience,* in 1912. He was called back to

Harvard University to succeed Professor George Herbert Palmer on his retirement in 1914. At Yale University I took an advanced course under Hocking titled Mysticism, and at Harvard I had his seminar and other advanced courses. I also served as his graduate assistant in an undergraduate course in ethics. Hocking was called back to Harvard especially to carry on the creative writing of the school of philosophy that had been so well and firmly established by Royce, and he later succeeded Royce in the Alford Chair of Philosophy.

Five of the essays assembled here were written in response to invitations from editors of special volumes. Dr. Marvin Farber, editor of *Philosophic Thought in France and the United States*, (University of Buffalo Publications in Philosophy, 1950), invited me to contribute an essay entitled "Philosophy of Religion in the United States in the Twentieth Century." The short essays, "Royce's Conception of God" and "Hocking's Conception of God" are extracted from that article.

The *In Memoriam* article on Hocking was written for *Philosophy and Phenomenological Research* at the invitation of the editor, Dr. Farber. It appeared in the March, 1967, number of the *Journal* (Vol. XXVII, pp. 461-466).

Professor Philippe Devaux, editor of the *Revue Internationale de Philosophie,* (Bruxelles 5, Belgique), invited me to write the essay "Royce's Contributions to Logic" for the special Royce volume issue of that international journal, which appeared in July, 1967. Containing full bibliographies of Royce's writing and of books and articles about him, as well as scholarly studies of Royce, this special number of the *Revue* is indispensable to the serious student of his works.

Professor LeRoy S. Rouner, editor of *Philosophy, Religion, and the Coming World Civilization, Essays in Honor of William Ernest Hocking,* (The Hague, Martinus Nijhoff, 1966), invited me to write the essay "Hocking's Contribution to Metaphysical Idealism." (See my account of this *Festschrift* volume in the *In Memoriam* essay.)

"Royce on the Origin and Development of Philosophical Terminology" is reprinted from *The Journal of Philosophy* (Vol. LIII, 1956, pp. 103-112). It is my contribution to a symposium in observation of the centennial of Royce's birth held at the December, 1955, annual meeting of the Eastern Division of the American Philosophical Association in Boston, Mass. I have appended to it the *Remarks* of the late Professor Harry Todd

Costello, which were later published in *The Journal of Philosophy* (Vol. LIII, pp. 311-313), under the title, "Royce's Encyclopedia Articles."

I reviewed Hocking's *Experiment in Education* for *Philosophy and Phenomenological Research* (Vol XV, March, 1955, pp. 424-426), and my review is reprinted here with a letter and extended comments of Hocking. I hope the publication of these remarks will result in a restudy of this too long neglected volume.

"Hocking and Marcel on Royce's Metaphysics" appears here for the first time. It indicates how the distinguished French philosopher, Dr. Gabriel Marcel, evaluates his relations to Royce and Hocking, and how Hocking estimates Marcel's *Royce's Metaphysics*. In the chapter entitled "Tillich and Marcel: Theistic Existentialists," in my *Crucial Issues in Philosophy*, I especially emphasized Marcel's acknowledged obligations to Royce and Hocking. To this chapter I have appended my review of the English translation of Marcel's highly significant *Royce's Metaphysics*.

Two of the essays and the sonnet included here are reprinted from my *Crucial Issues in Philosophy*. These are "Josiah Royce—California's Gift to Philosophy," "Hocking's Political Philosophy," and "To Josiah Royce," by Brent Dow Allinson.

Fortunately, annotated bibliographies of both authors are available, and detailed information about them will be found in the concluding section of the book titled *Bibliographies*. Some biographies are also listed.

"The Letters of Royce to William Torrey Harris" were edited by me with comments in *The Philosophical Forum* (Vol. XIII, 1955, Boston University). The originals are part of a large collection of letters written to William Torrey Harris and presented to the Hoose Library of Philosophy at the University of Southern California in 1953 by Miss Edith Davidson Harris, daughter of Dr. Harris, while I was serving as Director of the School of Philosophy.

When my "Josiah Royce—California's Gift to Philosophy" was published in *The Personalist* in 1950 (Vol. XXXI, pp. 352-368), I sent Mr. Stephen Royce, the elder son of Josiah Royce, a reprint. Later I sent him a copy of my edition of *Royce's Logical Essays*. This elicited from him the letters that are included here.

The Hocking Letters are selected from the many letters I have received from him during the past twenty years. Both the

Stephen Royce and Hocking letters are being deposited in the Hoose Library of Philosophy.

All of these letters contain biographical data of cardinal importance. For reference convenience they are numbered and arranged chronologically, and elucidative prefatory comments accompany each letter.

Most of the essays in this volume are concerned with the logical and metaphysical concepts and theories of the Royce-Hocking type of American idealism. But neither of them confined their interests to logic and metaphysics. Both were interested throughout their careers in the problems of philosophy of religion, ethics, and political philosophy. Consequently, many of their writings are concerned primarily with these problems. Royce's chief books in these fields are: *The Religious Aspect of Philosophy; The Conception of God; Studies of Good and Evil; The Conception of Immortality; The Philosophy of Loyalty; Race Questions, Provincialism, and Other American Problems; William James and Other Essays on the Philosophy of Life; The Problem of Christianity,* (2 vols.); *War and Insurance;* and *The Hope of the Great Community.*

Hocking's major works in the fields of philosophy of religion, ethics, and political philosophy are: *The Meaning of God in Human Experience: A Philosophic Study of Religion; Human Nature and Its Remaking; Morale and Its Enemies; Man and the State; The Self: Its Body and Its Freedom; The Spirit of World Politics: With Special Reference to the Near East; Rethinking Missions: A Layman's Inquiry after One Hundred Years; Thoughts on Death and Life; Living Religions and A World Faith; What Man Can Make of Man; Freedom of the Press: A Framework of Principle; Science and the Idea of God; Experiment in Education; The Coming World Civilization; The Meaning of Immortality in Human Experience;* and *Strength of Men and Nations.*

I commend all of these and the numerous other writings of Josiah Royce and William Ernest Hocking to the oncoming throng of college and university students everywhere. They will find them to be the best antidote to the now so widespread stream of philosophically sophisticated atheism. Undoubtedly this large stream of irreligion issues from the atheism of the dialectical materialism of Karl Marx and Friedrich Engels and their numerous ardent protagonists, and is fed by the atheistic existentialism of Jean Paul Sartre and his short-sighted followers.

I am deeply indebted to the above mentioned editors, Dr. Marvin Farber, Dr. LeRoy S. Rouner, Dr. Ph. Devaux, and to the editors of the *Journal of Philosophy* and *The Philosophical Forum* for permission to reprint the various essays and book reviews included herein. Complete references are given where each appears. I am also most grateful to Mr. Josiah Royce, son of Stephen Royce, and to Professor Richard Hocking for allowing me to publish here the Stephen Royce and Hocking Letters.

DANIEL S. ROBINSON

October 19, 1967

PART ONE

ESSAYS ON THE PHILOSOPHY OF JOSIAH ROYCE

I

JOSIAH ROYCE—CALIFORNIA'S
GIFT TO PHILOSOPHY

The fact that Josiah Royce was a Californian, more particularly the fact that the unique experiences which made him a Californian exercised the dominant influence in the shaping of his thought at the time that it was germinating, has not yet been adequately set forth and evaluated by any of the writers who have presumed to interpret the significance of his philosophy. It is true that credit is especially due to Professors J. Loewenberg and H. G. Townsend for having called attention to the value of Royce's California writings, but neither of them has developed an interpretation of his philosophy based upon his California experiences.[1] On the other hand, the almost complete ignoring of Royce's California writings by other chief interpreters, together with the widespread publicity that has been given to what, to say the least, is an entirely different and, I believe, erroneous interpretation of the significance of his philosophy, and, to say the most, has virtually now become a myth that has taken on additional accretions each time it has been repeated, has undoubtedly contributed to the neglect of Royce by the present generation of American students of philosophy. My main purpose here and now is to give a fresh and correct interpretation of the significance of his philosophy by exploiting the role that his being a Californian played in its development. But first let me dispose of those erroneous interpretations which, in their entirety, constitute what can properly be called the *Roycean myth*.

Presumably this myth was started by Professor George Santayana in his chapter on Royce in *Character and Opinon in the*

---

[1] See *Fugitive Essays by Josiah Royce*, edited and with an introduction by J. Loewenberg (Harvard University Press, Cambridge, 1920), pp. 3-37; and H. G. Townsend's *Philosophical Ideas in the United States* (American Book Company, Cincinnati, 1934), pp. 163f. See also Kurt F. Leidecker, *Josiah Royce and Indian Thought* (Kailas Press, New York, 1931).

17

United States (1920). His opinion is based upon his associations with Royce as teacher and colleague at Harvard and on the reading of some of his books, although he evidently did not read any of the writings on California. He begins by including Royce in "the genteel tradition." He says that he was "at home only in this circle of Protestant and German intuitionists," and that "pure transcendentalism" was his "technical method." Having thus stigmatized his colleague Santayana proceeds to deflate his reputation by underrating him. He writes: "His two thick volumes on *The World and the Individual* leave their subject wrapped in utter obscurity." "He resembled some great-hearted medieval peasant visited by mystical promptings." "In metaphysics as in morals Royce perpetually laboured the same points, yet they never became clear." "There was a voluminous confusion in his thought." "Royce slipped into a romantic equivocation which a strict logician would not have tolerated." "The good Royce was like a sensitive amateur refusing the role of villain, however brilliant and necessary to the play." One wonders what particular animus Royce must have aroused in his junior colleague that could have evoked such comments, but since he confesses that "you never caught him napping," it is fairly obvious that the brilliant and cocky young Santayana had come out second best in whatever tilts he had with Royce. His revenge was to publish a distorted account of his colleague in which he charged him with importing his philosophy from Germany and implied that he was lacking in original creative ability. Such obvious bias justifies our designating Santayana's Royce as the beginning of the Roycean myth.

To this myth Professor Ralph Barton Perry added considerably, although he does concede that Royce was an exceptional teacher. Primarily interested in exalting William James, he, doubtless unintentionally belittled Royce, so that his James is a veritable philosophical Gulliver and his Royce a puny Lilliputian metaphysician. It seems never to have occurred to Perry to question what Santayana wrote, and so he made no effort to correct his biased opinion of Royce. He implies that Royce was completely dependent upon James. Disregarding the fact that James was thirteen years older than Royce, and that they were in a teacher-student relationship at Johns Hopkins University, Perry writes: "During the years that elapsed before 1882, when he joined James at Harvard and became his neighbor and colleague it was to James that he continued to pour out his soul in long and frequent letters, and it was from James that he continued to receive the needed confirmation of his philosophical vocation." Perry emphasizes the fact that Royce "spent his early days in rude settlements which were conscious of the value of social life because as yet they possessed none," and adds that in his youth Royce was socially "disqualified even for the normal life of a pioneer community." On the other hand, James was always "at ease in every social situation." Here it should be especially noted that Perry completely ignores Royce's profound and penetrating analysis of how the pioneer mining communities of California developed into genuine social and law-abiding villages and cities, which probably means that he never studied Royce's California writings.

Carried away with the idea that contrasts are informative, Perry draws one after another. Here is one example: "While Royce wrote volumes to show that the lonely man needs society, James wrote articles to stress the fact that society needs loneliness." After stating that Royce "was in his day the most notable exponent of what Santayana called 'the genteel tradition',", Perry goes on to draw other interesting but misleading contrasts: "It thus transpired that, although Royce's was the characteristic American experience, it was left to James to develop an indigenous American philosophy, the first, perhaps, in which American experience escaped the stamp of an imported ideology. Royce, bred and reared amidst what was most unique and local in American life, imported his philosophy from the fashion makers of continental Europe; while James, uprooted almost from infancy and thoroughly imbued with the culture of Germany and France, was a philosophical patriot, cutting the garment of his thought from homespun materials and creating a new American model. Royce, the product of a raw pioneer community, conceived his universe as a perfected Absolute; James, nourished on the refinements and stabilities of advanced civilization, depicted a cosmic wilderness 'game-flavored as a hawk's wing.' "[2] By such admirably expressed contrasts Professor Perry perpetuated and enhanced the Roycean myth created by Santayana. Had he given the California writings the attention they deserved, he might have escaped this error. One thing these writings prove conclusively is that Royce was a true

[2] Ralph Barton Perry: *In the Spirit of William James* (Yale University Press, New Haven, 1938), pp. 25ff. For the quotations above see pp. 24, 13, and 5.

philosophical patriot as was James. If, as the proverb says, all comparisons are odious, so too are all contrasts, especially when they perpetuate and elaborate a myth.

Before Santayana wrote his opinion of Royce, Professor John Dewey attempted to drive a wedge between the earlier and later philosophy of the distinguished Californian by designating the former Critical Voluntarism and the latter Ontological Absolutism. He claims that between the year 1881 in his paper entitled "Kant's Relation to Modern Philosophical Progress" and 1885 in his *Religious Aspects of Philosophy,* Royce made a "transition from subordination of intellect to will to the reversed position."[3] Every serious interpreter of Royce recognizes that his philosophy continued to develop to the end of his life, but he himself would surely have denied that the old faculty psychology dichotomy between intellect and will was at all applicable to or compatible with his conception of the unity of the self, and he was in agreement with James in interpreting a self's conduct functionally. Although he does not mention Dewey, Perry really refutes Dewey's contention when he writes that Royce so intellectualized the will "that its victory over intellect is only a victory of intellect in one guise over intellect in another."[4] Although Dewey's penetrating analysis does throw considerable light on the development of Royce's philosophy, he undoubtedly magnifies and transforms what is rightly only a distinction of emphasis into two different philosophical positions. If we named what Dewey called Critical Voluntarism *Fichtean Absolutism* and what he called Ontological Absolutism *Hegelianism,* we can incorporate Dewey's analysis into the Roycean myth, although it is not fair to charge Dewey with having had any part in the invention of the myth. He wrote before Santayana and there is ample evidence that he had a genuine respect for Royce as a philosopher.

George H. Mead ended his article on Royce, James, and Dewey by elevating Dewey to the top rank.

"It is hardly necessary to point out that John Dewey's philosophy, with its statement of the end in terms of the means, is the developed method of that implicit intelligence in the minds of the American community. And for such an implicit intelli-

---

[3] See *Papers in Honor of Josiah Royce on his Sixtieth Birthday*, p. 17. Reprinted from *Philosophical Review*, Vol. XXV, No. 3 (Longmans, Green & Co., New York, 1916).

[4] *In the Spirit of William James, op. cit.,* p. 30.

gence there is no other test of moral and intellectual hypotheses except that they work. In the profoundest sense Dewey is the philosopher of America."[5]

To validate this conclusion Mead must dispose of Royce and James. We are not here concerned with his elimination of James, but his treatment of Royce definitely elaborates the Roycean myth, although he is more appreciative of Royce than Santayana or even Perry. He first dogmatically lays down the premise: "When the great speculative mind of Josiah Royce appeared in a California mining camp and faced the problems of good and evil, . . . he inevitably turned to the great philosophies of *outre mer,* in his dissatisfaction with the shallow dogmatism of the church and college of the pioneer."[6] Then he claims that the pioneer was unable to conceive of himself as "arising out of a society, so that by retiring into himself he could seize the nature of that society. . . . The communities came from him, not he from the community. And it followed that he did not hold the community in reverent respect."[7] Realizing that this general statement about pioneer society mentality was not strictly applicable to Royce, Mead continues with this assertion: "Notwithstanding Royce's intense moral sense and his passionate love of the community from which he came and to which he continued to belong, his philosophy belonged, in spite of himself, to culture and to a culture which did not spring from the controlling habits and attitudes of American society."[8] It is to be noted that this is really an unsupportable private opinion of Mead. He makes no appeal to the authority of Santayana. The chief argument he offers in proof of his thesis is strictly personal. He writes: "I can remember very vividly the fascination of idealisms in Royce's luminous presentation. They were part of that great world of *outre mer* and exalted my imagination as did its cathedrals, its castles, and all its romantic history. It was part of the escape from the crudity of American life, not an interpretation of it."[9] In such manner does Mead throw his support to the Roycean myth, apparently unaware that the application of the Freudian concept of escapism to Royce is com-

---

[5] *International Journal of Ethics,* Vol. 40 (University of Chicago Press, Chicago), p. 218. Compare Vol. 27, p. 231.

[6] *Ibid.,* p. 218. Compare Vol. 27, p. 168.

[7] *Ibid.,* p. 222.

[8] *Ibid.,* p. 223.

pletely at variance with his character, since he never tried to escape from anything.

Some general conclusions about the Roycean myth can now be drawn. It was created, nourished, and fostered by unsympathetic and hostile New Englanders who disregarded in its entirety the great evidential weight of the unique experiences that made Royce a Californian. Conceiving of an American pioneer community in terms of the social pattern of the British colonies, the makers of this myth overlooked the complexity of the social situation in the California of which Royce was a native son. After patient and painstaking investigations he wrote his *California* and this historical work will always be an indispensable source to every future historian of California. To this book he gave the subtitle *A Study of American Character*. The purveyors of the Roycean myth, who claim to be authorities in using the social pattern of a community to clarify its social philosophy, and without even taking the trouble to examine his writings on California, claim that Royce imported his philosophy from Germany. Whoever examines his monumental contributions on California will find in them sufficient data to refute the Roycean myth.

The California communities which were finally fused together to make the living culture peculiar to the state of California, whose early histories Royce so vividly portrays and interprets in his California writings, were especially complicated because the population consisted of easterners, southerners, Canadians, Mexicans, Spaniards, South Americans, Indians, some Frenchmen and scattering members of other races and nationalities. Due to the Mexican influence the dominant governing authority in the local communities was called *alcalde*. After the separation of California from Mexico each alcalde practically had to make his own law. Royce clearly describes the transition from this kind of law, through vigilante law, to a well-integrated communal life under the compulsion of the insistent demand for a state-wide constitutional law—which finally established order under the state government. Our contention is that his analysis of this social process is the ultimate source of his conception of the community which is so central in his whole philosophy. A more detailed analysis of Royce's California experiences and writings is required to defend this position.

---

[9] *Ibid.*, p. 223.

"Experience" is a multimeaning word. How would Royce have conceived of his California experiences? Since we propose to use these experiences to prove that he was an American philosopher, it is essential to state the sense in which he used the word "experience." In one of his most important essays, entitled "Tests of Right and Wrong" and published in 1880 while he was Instructor in English in the University of California, Royce gives an exceptionally clear statement of how he conceived of conscious experience. Each experiencing self, he argued, is in every moment of its existence conscious of a past that he acknowledges as real. Royce called this past the *positum* and the momentary experience of the self he named the *datum* (that which is given). But this conscious self also postulates a future which it expects and this is the *possible*. Now every conscious experience or, as Royce puts it:

". . . all conceivable truth is contained within the limits of the past, future, and possible experience of conscious beings. . . . Each moment of every life is judged in the presence of the whole of consciousness conceived as one being, or better, as one moment of being. Every moment-atom of this infinite life is approved if, knowing the other atoms, it recognized their claims in its action. For each deed of good done at any moment for another moment, the moral sense has the approving word that comes as it were from the very throne of the one infinite consciousness: Inasmuch as ye have done it unto the least of these, ye have done it unto me. This sense of the absolute worth of all experience, this insight into the unity of life, has been the continual theme of moral teaching and preaching, of all true religion, since there were minds to think."[10]

This, then, is what Royce meant by experience in 1880, and this became the cornerstone of all his philosophizing. He later elaborated this meaning of experience, but he never abandoned it.

Suppose we apply this conception to Royce's California experiences. It would mean that the waking hours he spent as a native-born citizen were filled with deeds that entered into the making of that spiritual and cultural whole which is California. His conscious life as lived in the communities of his native state forever belongs to the social phenomenon which goes by the

---

[10] *Fugitive Essays by Josiah Royce*, ed. by J. Loewenberg, *op. cit.*, pp. 203 and 217.

name of California. This is a part of Royce's social immortality. Most particularly it should be emphasized again that the numerous writings he penned about California are permanent ingredients of her cultural heritage. Surely this is the way Royce would have conceived of his California experiences. It is in full accord with his idealistic metaphysics to affirm that by his own deeds he wove himself into the state's cultural clothing so intricately, permanently and, as he would have said, eternally that the Roycean dyes can never be washed out of this royal garment. The concluding paragraph of his *California,* quoted below, is itself an eloquent affirmation of this metaphysical truth.

In clarifying the full meaning of Royce's California experiences, it is sufficient here barely to mention the essential biographical facts. Born in Grass Valley, a little north and west of Lake Tahoe in 1855, the only son of Josiah and Sarah Royce who had arrived in California in the Gold Rush of 1849, he received an elementary education in a school conducted by his mother and elder sisters in their own home. In 1866 Royce was sent to an academy in San Francisco. After completing the course of study there he entered the new University of California, and received the A.B. degree in 1875 at the age of twenty. On borrowed money he spent one year as a graduate student in German universities, and then was awarded a special fellowship at Johns Hopkins University, where he received the Ph.D. degree in 1878 when he was twenty-three. He returned to Berkeley as instructor in English at the University of California, and continued in this capacity until he was called to a position in philosophy at Harvard University in 1882. But he spent several months in California after he went to Harvard University doing research on his history of California, lecturing, and visiting with his mother and sisters.

This biographical sketch shows that Royce was under the influence of California for the first twenty-seven formative years of his life. It should be added that he early proved himself to be an intellectual genius. By the time he was thirty-two years of age Royce had completed all of his California writings. Here are the titles of these works: Senior essay on *Prometheus, Fugitive Essays, California from the Conquest in 1846 to the Second Vigilance Committee in San Francisco 1856* (published in 1886), *The Feud of Oakfield Creek: A Novel of California Life* (published in 1887), and *An Episode of Early California Life: The Squatter Riot of 1850 in Sacramento* (1885).

To these should be added an unusually important book which Royce induced his mother to write so that he could make use of it in writing his *California*. Here is the exact title: *A Frontier Lady, Recollections of the Gold Rush and Early California* (edited by R. H. Gabriel), by Sarah Royce. It was published in 1932.

Stating the bare facts of Royce's life in California and merely listing these writings is sufficient to prove that Royce was a California philosopher. Surely no one would question that these writings are major contributions to the culture of California. Royce gloried in the fact that he was a Californian. Professor Loewenberg has incorporated into his introduction to Royce's *Fugitive Essays* a beautifully expressed *Meditation Before the Gate*, in which the author depicts the effects produced in his consciousness as he viewed the Golden Gate and its environs from his study elevated "above the level of the lowlands." Referring to the philosophical problems with which he was wrestling at that time, the meditation closes with this striking sentence:

"With these problems I shall seek to bury myself earnestly, because that is each one's duty; independently, because I am a Californian, as little bound to follow mere tradition as I am liable to find an audience by preaching in this wilderness; reverently, because I am thinking and writing face to face with a mighty and lovely Nature, by the side of whose greatness I am but as a worm."[11]

Professor Loewenberg rightly comments that this meditation is that of a self-taught and self-conscious Californian.

What if he did utilize his knowledge of German philosophy in writing his early philosophical essays? From the earliest dawn of philosophy in the colonies and cities of ancient Greece every philosopher entitled to a place in the history of philosophy has had a knowledge of preceding philosophies. Shall we deny that Berkeley was a British philosopher because he knew and used the philosophy of Plato in developing his own philosophy; or that Kant was a German philosopher because he took Hume as a point of departure; or that Spinoza was a Dutch philosopher because he knew and used many of the ideas of Bruno and Plotinus? If a man is justly entitled to the high name of philosopher, and certainly Royce is as much entitled to be called

---

[11] *Ibid.*, p. 7.

a philosopher as any American, then his philosophy must perforce belong to and express the culture to which he belonged. In his introduction to the *Spirit of Modern Philosophy* Royce, himself, especially emphasized this truth. The conclusion, then, is that, being a Californian, Royce was perforce an American philosopher, and the argument is so far irrefutable.

However, this line of reasoning falls a little short of disposing of the central contention of the purveyors of the Roycean myth that his ethical idealism was imported from Germany and adapted to American life without having any real connection with our culture. To meet this fallacious and unproved assertion it is necessary to delve into Royce's California writings to find positive proof that his basic conceptions of the moral idea and of the community were derived from his interpretation of life as it was lived in the communities of California during the years dominated by the historic Gold Rush. These two conceptions are closely interwoven with his conception of experience, which has already been explained, and which constitutes the inner kernel of his metaphysics.

In an essay entitled "The Nature of Voluntary Progress" which was published in 1880, Royce argues that intellectual and moral progress results from "a change in the interests which men take in experience," and he says that the progress consists in expressing, simply and with as little effort as possible, "the new interests in terms of new or of old experience." He then elaborates each of these ideas under the headings, (a) *Progress as the Modification of Old Beliefs,* (b) *Voluntary Progress as the Formation of New Beliefs,* and (c) *Voluntary Progress with Change of Thought-Interest.* Applying this to industrial activities, he discusses division of labor and contends, against Plato and Aristotle, that "in differentiating social functions, surely we are not differentiating social aims" by which he denies that there are different virtues for different social functions. Royce next lays down as a general principle or law of social and political progress that whoever unites the efforts of men and thereby unifies labor simplifies the structure of society. Similarly political progress calls for a unification and harmonization of the desires of men by finding aims that are so comprehensive that they call forth all the energies of those who seek to realize them.

In Chapter IV of *California* Royce gives an excellent illustration of his social principle under the heading: *Pan and Cradle as Social Agents.* Here he shows in detail how the mining communities became more closely integrated when the mining tools changed from the pan to the cradle. And he makes these highly significant comments which prove that he fully understood the sociological import of this change. He writes:

"The great thing, however from the sociological point of view was that men now had voluntarily, and in an organized way, to work together. The miner's partnership, which grew up in this second stage of mining life, soon became one of the closest of California relationships, and, as such, has been widely and not unjustly celebrated in song and story. This accidental primitive society had passed from a state of 'nature' . . . and had become a collection of mutually more or less independent, but inwardly united bands. Rapidly as the successive stages of this growth passed by, they still left their mark on the social order."

In the following section titled *The Beginning of Sluice Mining,* Royce shows how this socializing process resulting from a division of labor was carried much further by placer mining. Here again Royce says: "The introduction of the sluice, with its various auxiliaries . . . acted indirectly on society, as a check to the confusion and disorder. . . . Sluice mining meant serious responsibilities of many sorts, and so, in the end, good order."[12] It is evident that this is the germ of Royce's conception of the community, for these examples show just how that conception emerged from his idea of social progress. The significance of this idea for Royce's conception of the community is discussed more fully below.

Royce concludes his exposition of the moral ideal with this statement: "In an ideal state every one would give himself up to whatever work were before him, every one would feel that the world's ends were his ends, and no human will would be coerced by another, because perfect submission would be the attitude for everyone." He says that this is just like the socialist ideal, and that both ideals are "alike impractical, and alike useful as ideals." And why are they impractical? Because, as Royce freely admits, "Unrest, dissatisfaction, is an eternal part of conscious life. I see no reason for being confident that good will ever triumph over evil in more than a very restricted sense," and he

---

[12] Josiah Royce: *California from the Conquest in 1846 to the Second Vigilance Committee in San Francisco 1856—A Study of American Character* (Alfred A. Knopf, New York, 1948, reprinted from the original edition of 1886), pp. 227 and 244.

adds that "if at any moment there were triumph we could not be certain of its permanence." Yet "there is no reason why we should on that account work less vigorously, or make our aims less lofty. It is a cowardly soul that needs the certainty of success before it will work. It is a craven who despairs and does nothing because what he can do may turn out a failure."[13]

To this brief summary of Royce's conception of the moral ideal, as he formulated it in 1880 while he was an Instructor in English at the University of California, let me add a fine passage from his novel of California life entitled *The Feud of Oakfield Creek*. Here he puts his conception of the moral idea into the mouth of his hero, Professor Escott:

Harold: "I am to live for—I know not what!"

Professor Escott: "Live to hold on and fight, my boy! What have I lived for? You know my doctrines as well as I do. The Great Spirit needs brave children. We are all of us poor specimens of what he's looking for. But, alas! he can make us no better. For if it were he that made us better, we should be worth nothing. We alone can give ourselves the bravery that he wants. And so, bad as we are, our game is his game, if we only stand up to it, and fight for our side. That's the whole story of life. The man that demands more of life than that is a fool. The man who, by chance, gets more is fortune's spoiled child, who's like as not all the worse for his good luck. This seems a little dreary, at odd minutes, when a fellow has neuralgia, or feels worn out, but it's God's truth. The world is the home of brave men, and the prison of cowards. That's all I can see in it. Apart from that chance to be a brave fellow, in a good cause, and for one's friends, what is there after all?"[14]

Thus we find here in two of Royce's California writings early statements of the moral ideal which he later expressed in much greater detail in his *Studies of Good and Evil* (1898) and in his *Philosophy of Loyalty* (1908). And here we find the germ of his solution of the problem of evil which he set forth in Part Two of his *Spirit of Modern Philosophy* (1892) and in his *The Problem of Christianity,* two volumes, (1913).

---

[13] *Fugitive Essays, op. cit.,* pp. 116, 125, 128, 129, 131f.

[14] Josiah Royce: *The Feud of Oakfield Creek* (Houghton, Mifflin Co., Boston, 1887), p. 437. See *Fugitive Essays, op. cit.,* p. 131 for an earlier (1880) statement of this creed: "It is a cowardly soul that needs the certainty of success before it will work. It is a craven who despairs and does nothing because what he can do may turn out a failure."

Royce's moral ideal as developed in his California writings is really identical with the idea of the community when this is taken in its widest sense. However, in his essay on "Voluntary Progress" he clearly distinguishes four chief types of voluntary social activities. These are: "(1) thought activities; (2) industrial activities: (3) political activities; (4) and moral activities." He says that all of these social activities are characterized by the fact that "a concert of individual actions produces a resultant greater than the numerical sum of the individual contributions, or else different in kind from this sum." Regarding the state he writes: "The resultant of united political activity is again the state, an institution different in kind from the contributions brought by any one member of society, whose power is therefore not the mere arithmetical sum of the powers of its subjects, but an organic product of all of them."[15] Further on he differentiates industrial, political, and moral activities in this fashion:

"Industrial activities are the expression of the interest in supplying the physical wants of individuals. They are the most direct expressions in society of the instinct of self-preservation. Political activities represent the same interest on a higher plane of intelligence, with more foresight and more understanding of the way in which self-preservation is to be furthered by the use of force. Moral activities result from an extended interest in conscious life as such, and express a desire for the preservation and bettering of living beings because they are living beings, and not because they are important to one's self."[16]

Now this implies that there are four kinds of communities determined by these four kinds of social activities, and it also implies that there are different grades or stages of development of each. We might name these: (1) Economic and Industrial Social Organizations; (2) Political Societies; (3) Cultural Social Organizations; and (4) Moral Communities, of which Royce in *The Problem of Christianity* took the church to be the best example. Obviously these all coalesce in his final conception of the great community.

We have aready quoted passages from Royce's *California* to show that he recognized various stages in the evolution of the

---

[15] *Fugitive Essays, op. cit.*, pp. 111f. For a more detailed statement of the functioning of these activities in the community see *The Religious Aspect of Philosophy* (1885), pp. 211-223, where these activities are closely integrated with the moral ideal.

[16] *Ibid.*, pp. 124f.

mining towns while they were primarily industrial communities. That his own experience and knowledge of these growing communities was a primary source of his general theory of the community is proved by the confession Royce makes in the conclusion of his *California*. He has especially indicated in Chapter IV entitled "The Struggle for Order" how the mad scramble and ceaseless struggles of the pioneers to get gold for themselves produced vicious social evils in each mining center, and these very evils forced the higher-minded men to organize a political society or community that could correct outlawry and establish order. And so he concludes that the whole lesson of the Californian's early history when rightly read—

". . . is a lesson in reverence for the relations of life. It was by despising or at least by forgetting them that the early community entered into the valley of the shadow of death; and there was salvation for the community in those days only by virtue of its final and hard-learned submission to what it had despised and forgotten. This lesson, I confess, has come home to me personally, as I have studied this early history, with a quite unexpected force. I had always thought of the old days as times of fine and rough labors, amusements, and crimes, but not as a very rational historical process: I have learned, as I have toiled for a while over the sources, to see in these days a process of divinely moral significance. And as a Californian I am glad to be able to suggest what I have found, plain and simple as it is, to any fellow Californian who may perchance note in himself the faults of which I make confession. Here in the early history are these faults, writ large, with their penalties, and the only possible salvation for them.

"After all, however, our lesson is an old and simple one. It is the State, the Social Order, that is divine. We are all but dust, save as this social order gives us life. When we think it our instrument, our plaything, and make our private fortunes the one object, then this social order rapidly becomes vile to us; we call it sordid, degraded, corrupt, unspiritual, and ask how we may escape from it forever. But if we turn again and serve the social order, and not merely ourselves, we soon find that what we are serving is simply our own highest spiritual destiny in bodily form. It is never truly sordid or corrupt or unspiritual; it is only that we are so when we neglect our duty."[17]

Here we have the source of Royce's conception of the great community. He forged it out of his California experiences. He did not import it from Germany. His speech on the sinking of the *Lusitania* shows how intensely he could despise the alien community that turned against the great community of human civilized society. In this is all the patriotic fervor of the Vigilantes who established law and order in California. Royce was a native of California, who more than any other of her citizens of his time comprehended the travails and sorrows of her birth, and correctly interpreted the historical process through which she achieved the status of an American Commonwealth. That he became recognized at Harvard University as the dominant philosopher of the United States was due more to what his California experiences meant to him than to any other single force.

Royce fully repaid his obligation to James in his Phi Beta Kappa address by naming him as one of the three greatest American philosophers, the other two being Jonathan Edwards and Ralph Waldo Emerson. He based his opinion on the fact that only these three won a world-wide, and especially European, attention. We must agree with Professor Howison when he excludes both Emerson and James from this high honor on the ground that Emerson was a moral sage and poet rather than a philosopher, while James was a great prose writer and psychologist who subordinated argument to felt wishes. This conclusion of Howison will, I believe, be the judgment of history:

"If the list of strictly philosophic thinkers in our country, rightly headed by Jonathan Edwards ... is now to be continued, it is little to be questioned that the place of our colleague (Royce) in such quiet and natural, though indeed unavoidable, self-forgetfulness, assigned to his gifted friend James, really belongs to himself."[18]

Just as New England's gift to philosophy, Jonathan Edwards, is generally conceded the title of the foremost American philosopher of our colonial history, so California's gift to philosophy, Josiah Royce, will eventually receive the recognition he so well deserves as the foremost American philosopher of our national history.

When I completed this essay and delivered it as a lecture on a Philosophy Forum Program at the University of Southern

---

[17] *California from the Conquest in 1846 to the Second Vigilance Committee in San Francisco 1856, op. cit.*, p. 393.

[18] *Josiah Royce Papers, op. cit.*, p. 15.

California in the autumn of 1949, it ended with the preceding paragraph. Now as I reprint it here, I feel constrained to add a brief comment in explanation of my criticism of Ralph Barton Perry's contribution to what I have named the Roycean myth. When I was a graduate student in philosophy at Harvard, I learned as much or more from Perry's advanced courses than I learned from those of Royce, Hocking, and Hoernlé, with whom I was more in sympathy. I served as Perry's graduate student assistant in his history of philosophy course at Radcliffe College. He befriended me in many ways, and I have always held him in the highest esteem.

After he completed his monumental Pulitzer Prize biography: *The Thought and Character of William James,* which is unquestionably one of the best biographies in the English language, I invited Perry in 1937 to deliver the Second Series of Lectures on the Mahlon Powell Foundation at Indiana University. He chose as a title for these lectures *In the Spirit of William James.* Being a sequel to his biographical work, this is one of his best books. Yet in it he made his contribution to the Roycean myth! Why?

The answer is that Perry was a bosom friend of William James. He properly exalted and upgraded James, who can hardly be overpraised. But in doing this Perry had a tendency, which was probably unconscious, to downgrade Royce. Sometimes he forgot that James was also a bosom friend of Royce. Nevertheless, in the author's opinion Perry refutes himself. In Volume II of *The Thought and Character of William James,* he reprints in Appendix V an extended dialogue between James and Royce, entitled "Discussion of the Absolute." Any competent impartial judge who fully comprehends the philosophies of these two bosom friends must admit that Royce comes out the winner in this famous dialogue.

I doubt whether James or Perry ever delved quite as deep in metaphysics as did Royce, and I doubt whether Mead and Santayana ever did either. James was a greater psychologist than Royce, but Royce was a greater logician and metaphysician. But if, as Sir Roger de Coverly said, all comparisons are odious, then a comparison between two such philosophical geniuses as William James and Josiah Royce is doubly odious. I fully recognize that all of these thinkers were supermen intellectually. Each has left writings that are permanent and intrinsically valuable contributions to the literature of philosophy.

TO JOSIAH ROYCE

BY

BRENT DOW ALLINSON

"The Great Spirit needs brave children—We alone can give ourselves the bravery that he wants—That's the whole story of life. . . . The world is the home of brave men, and the prison of cowards." Josiah Royce, in *The Feud of Oakfield Creek.*

Seaward he set his course, nor hugged the shore
Of circumstance, resolved, dauntless to sound
The pure unfathomable seas — explore
The mind's rich caverns measureless, profound,
Sense that which lies below, beyond, behind
The knower and the known; — and when the West
Was fenced with fear and golden greed to find
The foam-reefed Isles of Hesperus, the blest!

Teach me your secret O brave mariner,
That when my tides of faith are all but spent,
When night and freezing winds afflict the sea,
When, though at home I am a foreigner
And homesick, I may somehow learn content,
And find the pole-star of your loyalty![1]

---

[1] 1955 being the Centennial Year of his birth, this sonnet is here re-published as a memorial to Professor Royce by special permission of the author, Brent Dow Allinson. Now slightly revised by the author, it was awarded the Lloyd McKim Garrison Prize, and silver medal, by the Department of English, in Harvard College, at Commencement, 1917, shortly after the death of Professor Royce.

Brent Dow Allinson explained to me the circumstances of his writing and rewriting this sonnet, in a letter from which I quote with his permission. "As a youthful eye-witness of the momentous events of the closing days of Royce's life at Harvard, (and an editor of *The Harvard Monthly*, in its last year of existence), your article in *The Personalist* has a memory-evoking quality for me, revives very keen emotions . . . . During the course of that winter, the Department of English at Harvard announced the theme of its annual prize-award for original English poetry:— 'Josiah Royce' . . . . There were a good many manuscripts submitted, as I recall it, to Dean Briggs; and my astonishment and gratification were raised to the zenith of a youth's consciousness, when it was announced that a sonnet which I had worked on for a good many days and nights, and had submitted in January or February of that winter, was given the poetry prize, shortly after our formal declaration of a state of war with imperial Germany.

"It occurs to me that you might care to read it, now, and perhaps publish it as an evocation by your article. I have revised a few words of it, which I think is the privilege of a creative writer—and attached as a superscription a few lines that seem to me to heighten its effect—from your quotation from Royce's novel, which I have never otherwise read. The sonnet was published originally in *The Harvard Monthly*, I think, and in my own small volume of poems entitled: *Youth and the Singing Shadows*, (Chicago, 1922)."

II

ROYCE ON THE ORIGIN AND DEVELOPMENT OF PHILOSOPHICAL TERMINOLOGY

Josiah Royce contributed four articles on philosophical terminology to Baldwin's *Dictionary of Philosophy and Psychology*. They are entitled *Greek Terminology, Latin and Scholastic Terminology, Kant's Terminology,* and *Hegel's Terminology*. Each article is initialed J. R., and the list of authors states that these initials stand for Josiah Royce. Royce also contributed seven other articles to Baldwin's *Dictionary,* but these four, totaling approximately 35,000 words, are much longer than the other seven. In several respects, they constitute a unified whole. Written in his inimitable style, they contain Royce's theory of the origin and the stages in the development of philosophical terminology, as well as his idea of its relation to special systems of philosophy.

The opening sentence of each article clearly indicates its scope. In parentheses after the title, *Greek Terminology,* is the statement "(considered in relation to Greek philosophy)," and following the title, *Latin and Scholastic Terminology,* is this statement "with reference principally to Patristic and Scholastic philosophy and to Thomism." Thus, these two articles contain Royce's theory of the origin and of the development of philosophical terminology in Ancient and Medieval Western Philosophy. In parentheses following the title, *Kant's Terminology,* is the statement "(in relation to the Kantian Philosophy)," and in parentheses after the title, *Hegel's Terminology,* appears the statement "(in relation to the Hegelian Philosophy)." Thus, these two articles rest upon the evident assumption that the philosophical terminology of a special author is shaped by his own philosophical system. This assumption is also operative throughout the other two articles.

All four of these articles are of the highest quality, and they are sufficient in themselves to establish their author's reputation as a philosophical scholar of the highest rank. They prove his mastery of Greek, Latin, and German as working tools. They demonstrate his wide and intimate knowledge of the extensive literature involved in a scholarly discussion of philosophical terminology over such a long period of the history of Western culture, and they are enriched throughout by the originality of his philosophical insights. He does not hesitate to point out erroneous ideas of commentators, and he repeatedly makes original shrewd observations that throw a flood of light on the subject under discussion. Although they have been unduly neglected, these four articles richly deserve the careful study of every student of philosophy. My purpose is to demonstrate these judgments by giving a summary of Royce's exposition.

The Pre-Socratic Greek philosophers began by taking words that were in daily use as the names of certain aspects of the physical world. This was quickly modified in two ways. For those aspects of the physical world which were not familiar to the populace the philosophers coined new terms. Royce says this is a perennial accompaniment of abstract thought, and was quite pronounced among the Pythagoreans. Another device was to give existing words new meanings by taking them out of their context and changing them into technical terms. He cites Anaximander's term, (the Boundless) as an early example of this method of building a philosophical terminology, and he says that it is a good example of a term whose meaning is not clear since he may have meant either boundless in the sense of originating new products, or boundless in its extent. Such terms have, Royce remarks, "indeed, too much of the boundless about them." He next considers the tendency for terms to *alter their meaning* as a philosopher uses them. The ordinary terms cannot convey the philosopher's more precise meanings, and thus his thought tends to transform whatever he touches. He uses the expression of Heraclitus, (fire ever-living) to exemplify this tendency, and also the Eleatic term *being*. He writes: "From the Eleatic philosophers down, and very notably in Plato's ontological dialogues, such as the *Parmenides,* the *Sophist,* and the *Philebus,* this is what happens to the terms used for being."

At this stage in the development of philosophical terminology, each philosopher begins to employ special devices for setting up contrasts between his own use of a term and that of popular speech. Sometimes he criticises popular usage for its ambiguity, and sometimes he suggests substitutions. Thus, there is an intentional adjustment of terms to the philosopher's doctrines, as when Parmenides denies the possibility of speaking truly of "non-being," or when Empedocles denies that mortal things have either an origin or an end because they are all mixtures of what is mixed. This is where the history of philosophical terminology proper begins. Thus, according to Royce, it is not until a philosopher deliberately begins to adjust his terms to his own doctrines that a genuine philosophical terminology can be said to exist. Now this is found in Parmenides, Empedocles, and Anaxagoras, but not in the earlier Pre-Socratic philosophers.

The Sophists, and Socrates, Plato, and Aristotle attained a still higher stage in the development of philosophical terminology when they made the effort to define terms a major part of the philosophic enterprise itself. From henceforth clarifying ideas and defining terms develop side by side and in the Platonic dialogues the method of dialectics becomes a conscious art. Among other intellectual activities this involves the use of classification and division of terms, and their arrangement in an hierarchy. But this very hierarchical arrangement and art of dialectics requires the coinage of new terms to fill gaps, and also to name the various intellectual processes that are involved in the dialectical method itself. Nevertheless, Plato's terminology remains "incipient, tentative, transitional," and he always applies it afresh and is not bound in any given context by terms he may have used in any previous analysis he may have made.

Aristotle, on the other hand, deliberately attempted to correlate terminology with the ideal of a philosophical system. He undertook to name the different sciences, thus technically distinguishing the various aspects of things. Royce says that Aristotle attempted to solve *"fundamental problems by means of this method of distinctions."* In using this method Aristotle was consciously attempting *"to harmonize the various points of view* of earlier thinkers, and *to solve apparent contradictions* by showing how in 'a certain sense' each of two apparently contradictory propositions can be true." He appeals to general usage, but consciously purifies and alters it. Royce discusses in some detail Eucken's analysis of Aristotle's terminology, using specific terms which, he says, "are all classic instances of the evolution of terminology in Aristotle through sharper differentiations of expressions and of meanings." This explains why philosophy owes to Aristotle "a very large portion of its later technical terminology," a debt that is especially obvious and well-known in logic.

Royce concludes his account of Greek Terminology with an account of what the Post-Aristotelian philosophers contributed to the development of philosophical terminology. He gives special emphasis to the contributions of the Stoics. He specifically mentions five important principles that help to explain these later additions to and modifications of terminology. The first is *"the growth of a clearer consciousness as to the inner life, and as to the contrast between the objective and subjective aspects of reality."* Examples of this principle are to be found in the Stoic doctrines of the emotions, and the practical aspects of mental life. A second principle that influenced later Greek terminology is *"the relations between philosophy and the now more or less independent developments of the special sciences,* such as medicine." Examples of this are the doctrine of the temperaments, which was systematized by Galen, and the doctrine of the *"pneuma or vital spirit"* in Galen and the Stoics. A third principle is the growing importance of *"the problems of theology* viewed as such." As an example of this, Royce cites the doctrine of the *logos,* originated by Heraclitus, but developed by the Stoics and by Philo. A fourth aspect of later Greek terminology is its concern with more purely *ethical concepts.* Examples of this are the Stoic ideal of *"the concordant or consistent life"* (life in accordance with nature), and the concept of the indifferent over against what is good and evil. The fifth aspect is *logic,* the terminology of which was especially enriched by the Stoics. They coined the technical name *logic,* made a revision of Aristotle's categories, and created a new terminology for various kinds of judgments, including hypothetical judgments.

Summarizing Royce's conclusions in the article entitled "Greek Terminology," we can say that by the end of the Hellenistic Period of Greek philosophy the development of philosophical terminology had evolved through these three stages: (1) The Pre-Critical Stage in which philosophers used terms from popular speech, but modified them to make them convey a new meaning, and also coined new terms when this became necessary. (2) The Critical Stage in which philosophical terms were deliberately correlated with philosophical systems and term-making became a conscious art. This second stage culminated in Aristotle. (3) A Third Stage is found in the Post-Aristotelian Hellenistic Philosophy where there is an extensive elaboration and enrichment of philosophical terminology in accordance with the five principles already formulated and exemplified. Royce ends his discussion of the origin and development of philosophical terminology among the Greeks with a valuable summary in the form of bibliographical comments on the literature which he had consulted in writing the article, and with a *Glossary* of Greek terms.

In his article entitled *Latin and Scholastic Terminology,* Royce especially stresses the influence of Aristotle on the Scholastics, which goes back to the translations and commentaries of Boethius and was developed in its most finished form by St. Thomas and his followers. He shows how the schoolmen elaborated the Aristotelian and Platonic usage. For example, they formulated so many definitions of the term *being,* Royce writes, as to "form an undoubtedly difficult, not to say over-wealthy collection of terms for expressing the various aspects and types of being." He reviews these various meanings in considerable detail, showing how the noun *ens* and the verb *esse* each had several different meanings, and how such Aristotelian terms as essence and substance, formal and material, and potentiality and actuality were all elaborated in such an exact manner as to make the terms used "formally exact, but materially very arbitrary and unenlightening." He also gives many examples of the psychological vocabulary of the scholastics to supplement his analysis of their metaphysical vocabulary. It is obviously impossible here to give a detailed account of his penetrating analysis of Scholastic terminology. But Royce's final conclusion is especially worthy of note: "These illustrations of the metaphysical and psychological vocabulary of scholasticism tend to throw light upon the origin, and the general character of this terminology. . . . The central character of the whole scholastic vocabulary remains its elaborate use of *distinctions.* The method of distinctions had already been carried far by Aristotle. He used it to solve apparent contradictions, and so to prepare the way for synthetic views of his world. Scholasticism made the method of distinctions more and more an ideal." This article ends with a *Glossary* of the Latin terms discussed by the author.

Royce begins his exposition of Kant's philosophical Terminology by pointing out an important contrast between modern and Greek thinkers with respect to terminology. With the Greeks, he writes, "The power of mere tradition was at its minimum. Creation was relatively free." But with the moderns "an elaborate, and in fact often extremely difficult terminology, the result of several successive great movements of human thought—the terminology of Scholasticism—stood in the way of novelty of expression." Locke undertook to break completely with tradition and as a result there is "a certain disorganization of technical language, which upon occasion, give to his terms a capricious seeming, without freeing them altogether from the influence of the past." As an example, Royce cites Locke's use of the term *substance*.

When we consider Kant the situation is far more complex and problematic, Royce contends. He had to appeal to tradition and yet he is not content to accept either the scholastic terminology or that of Wolff, for he shares Locke's conscious revolt against traditional terms that would bind and restrict his thought. Consequently, he tries to select and to adapt traditional philosophical terms to suit his own purpose. Yet he follows no single principle in doing this, and seems often to be dissatisfied with the effort he has made. Thus, he frequently changes the meaning of his terms in the course of the same discussion. Royce comments: "His usage in such cases seems to be in a sort of Heraclitean flux, so that we do not twice step into the same river of expression while we wander in search of the thought." I know of no more succinct explanation of the difficulties involved in trying to understand what Kant meant by his technical terms.

Royce gives a detailed account of various treatises dealing with Kant's terminology. He says that Kant's own formal definitions of his terms are seldom to be taken as final. Kant "is a great lover of analysis; so that while, like Aristotle and the Scholastics, he makes systematic use of the method of distinctions for the sake of explaining or removing the contradictions of thought and opinion, he is much more radical than any of his predecessors in the distinctions that he draws, and his world largely consists of definable barriers and chasms. Kant loves, meanwhile, synthesis, but is never as successful in this direction as in the other." With these cogent remarks, Royce proceeds to discuss Kantian terminology by considering the contrast between philosophical terms, and those of mathematics, and of the empirical sciences. He gives a good deal of attention to Kant's psychological terms, and also to his epistemological terms, into the details of which we cannot enter here. The article concludes with a useful *Glossary* of the Kantian terms he has discussed.

Royce's article on *Hegel's Terminology* rounds out and completes his general theory of the origin and development of philosophical terminology. He begins the discussion with a section entitled "General Nature and Origin of Hegel's Terminology." Kant influenced Hegel's terminology in two ways. Some of his technical terms are borrowed directly from Kant. But other terms that were borrowed from earlier sources which had also been employed by Kant, are much influenced by the Kantian usage. On the whole, however, we must not think of Hegel's terminology as being primarily Kantian in its origin because he worked out a relatively independent terminology which was on the whole adequate to his complex philosophical system. Royce thinks that Hegel's terms are frequently decidedly novel and that they are chosen "with a very careful regard to his own central theories."

Hegel thinks that this method of formulating a technical vocabulary for a philosophical system is justified by being a general practice among the outstanding philosophers of the past. We have already learned from the study of Greek terminology that "the deliberate employment of an already familiar term in a meaning which is not only specialized, but specialized through an emphasis laid upon tendencies or purposes latent in the popular usage" was a basic method used by Greek thinkers in creating their technical vocabulary. But Royce points out that two significant facts make Hegel's employment of this method quite different and far more baffling than was its employment by the Greeks. In Hegel's case (1) "the terms whose sense is thus transformed are already old technical terms of a past usage no longer vague but as Hegel himself holds, rather too abstractly sharp in definition," and (2) "the change from the traditional usage is frequently very considerable, and concerns some of the most original features of the Hegelian system." Consequently a superficial knowledge of the terminology of Hegel can be extremely misleading, as is exemplified by various erroneous criticisms of his system.

In particular, Royce mentions four erroneous criticisms that rest upon such a superficial misinterpretation of Hegel's terminology. These are: (1) That Hegel's philosophy is a panlogism, (2) that he reduces life to mere thought, (3) that he recognizes "no reality but the thinking process," and (4) that he identifies "the philosophizing intelligence with the absolute." To avoid such errors Royce says it is necessary to summarize the whole of Hegel's *Logik* in order to restate his definitions accurately.

He points out that Hegel often gives his own etymologies of the terms he uses and these are sometimes quite arbitrary. He is also fond of plays upon words. *Hegel's Terminology* in its technical form appears first in the *Phänomenologie des Geistes,* but in its richest and fullest forms in the *Logik* and the *Encyclopädie der Philosophischen Wissenschaften.* In the *Phenomenology* many of his basic terms are not used in the way they are used in the later works, and many terms there used are not employed in the later works. Consequently, the understanding of Hegel's terminology in its final and complete form depends on a thorough knowledge of the later works.

The second section of this article is entitled "Fundamental Features of the System as Determining the Terminology." Royce here states what he regards as the three central theories which constitute the "distinguishing features of Hegel's doctrine." The first thesis is "that the factor usually called experience and the other factor (Kant's spontaneity of the thinking process) can never be sundered, but are universally present in all grades of knowledge, however low or high." The second thesis is "that the lower stages of the knowing process itself are identical in their essential nature with the higher so that the various grades of knowledge usually distinguished as *perception, understanding, reason,* etc., are not essentially different mental processes but are merely successive phases in the evolution of a single process." And the third thesis is "that the knowing process in these its phases, in its evolution, and in its entire constitution, not only precisely corresponds to, but is identical with, the essential nature of the world, the object or true being, which is known." Royce then goes on to illustrate how these three theses determine the meaning of Hegel's basic categories such as *Sein, Dasein, Existenz, Ding, Eigenschaft,* etc., He writes: "The term *Reflection* is an interesting example of a term which first suggests to the reader's mind the process of subjective reflection, while Hegel frequently emphasizes its objective meaning as a name for a real process." This explains why Hegel's technical terminology is so difficult for a student to grasp.

The third section of the article on *Hegel's Terminology* is entitled *The Dialectical Method: General Features,* and it is especially important because of the distinction which Royce makes between the two different forms this method takes in Hegel's system. He emphasizes the fact that Hegel did not originate either form of the method. They rest on two principles that are deeply rooted in the history of philosophy. These are (1) *"that facts are knowable only as related,"* and (2) *"that the universal laws of ideal processes, taken together with the processes which embody these laws, are equivalent to all that is properly to be meant by reality."* Hegel developed these two principles with great thoroughness and originality, Royce claims.

Hegel's first form of the dialectical method applies to categories that are so abstract as to be ambiguous in their meaning. When rightly criticised and understood these defective categories, which are those of immediacy, lead to higher categories. The process of criticising them and of transforming them into higher categories is the first form of the dialectical method. Royce gives a single example from the *Phänomenologie.* Common sense, when asked to point out an object that is certain may say *"This object, viz.,* the object that I here and now see or touch: *This is known to me directly."* But Hegel asks: *"What is this object?* What does *this* mean?" And then he shows that such knowledge is so vague, general, and indefinite as to refer to anything whatever, and hence its meaning is "as good as nothing."

The second form of the dialectical method refers to a much higher stage of reflection than that of common sense, the stage, namely, where a philosopher has already accepted the relativity of our world and has become a sceptic with respect to there being any objective meaning, beyond his own subjective state of mind. In this case the dialectical method consists of three stages. First, such a philosopher is forced to acknowledge that any ideal construction requires for its formulation a certain set of ideas or concepts, a, b, c, d, etc. Secondly, he has to ask whether there is any objective truth that corresponds to this intellectual requirement that has to be met if he is to think at all. And thirdly, he has to admit that, if he has consistently evaluated the system, it must itself be real, so that "the fully grown *Begriff* is itself the object sought, the curtain is the picture, and the thought is the being." It is this second form of the dialectical method which Royce himself accepted when in the *Principles of Logic* he laid down and italicised this fundamental proposition: "There are certain modes of activity, certain laws of the rational will, which we reinstate and verify, through the very act of attempting to presuppose that these modes of activity do not exist, or that these laws are not valid."[1] This, in my opinion, is a central thesis of any and of every idealistic metaphysics, but it should be emphasized that Royce's precise wording of it is quite unique.

Following his exposition of these two forms of the dialectical method, Royce discusses in considerable detail the various technical terms which Hegel employs in his system under three general headings. These are (1) *The Most General Terms of the System; Experience of the Dialectic Process.* (2) *Further General Terminology. The Stages of the Development of "Vermittelung,"* and (3) *Other Terms.* Time does not permit us to go into these details. The article ends with a useful *Glossary* of the various terms of the Hegelian system, the meanings of which Royce has explained in the course of the article.

Concluding, now, with a final evaluation, I think it will be generally conceded that these four articles on Greek, Latin, Kantian, and Hegelian philosophical terminology reveal Josiah Royce at his best. They are packed full of technical information covering almost all of the history of Western philosophy, and they demonstrate that their author was, in the fullest sense of the word, a philosopher's philosopher. Students will do well to explore this rich store of semantic material.[2]

---

[1] See D. S. Robinson, Editor, *Royce's Logical Essays* (W. C. Brown Company, Dubuque, Iowa, 1951) pp. 364f. On Royce's philosophy, see also J. Harry Cotton, *Royce on the Human Self* (Harvard University Press, Cambridge, Mass., 1954); John E. Smith, *Royce's Social Infinite* (The Liberal Arts Press, New York, 1950); and D. S. Robinson, *Crucial Issues in Philosophy* (Christopher Publishing House, Boston, Mass., 1955) chapters XVI, XVII.

[2] Reprinted from the *Journal of Philosophy*, Vol. LIII, 1956, pp. 103-112.

III

COSTELLO'S "ROYCE'S ENCYCLOPEDIA ARTICLES"

Professor Harry Todd Costello attended the meeting of the Eastern Division of the American Philosophical Association, at which the above paper was read, and he made some informative and interesting extemporaneous remarks which he later revised and published in the *Journal of Philosophy* (Vol. LIII, April 26, 1956, pp. 311-313) under the title "Royce's Encyclopedia Articles." With the permission of the editor they are reprinted here.

Royce's Encylopedia Articles[1]

The first time I ever heard Royce was soon after the turn of the century. He came to our high school auditorium one afternoon at four, to lecture to the townspeople. My Sunday School teacher was distressed later. "He was using the simplest words, but it was the way he was putting them together." I forgot the main argument, but remember a joke. A mother says to her daughter, "Why *do* you always contradict what I say?" To which the daughter answers, "Why, mother dear, I never do." I know the lecture was castigating pragmatism, and it seems to me he used the illustration I heard from his lips several times in later years. The pragmatists say "the true is what works." An Irishman wrote an angry letter to another man, with uncomplimentary references to the man's mother. A friend tried to dissuade him from sending it. "What do you know about his mother?" "Yis, but it'll worrk. If he has a shpark of manhood

---

[1] This paper is an extempore comment, revised later with some additions, on Daniel Robinson's paper, read at the American Philosophical Association meeting at Boston University, December 29, 1955, which concerned Royce's article on terminology, in Baldwin's *Dictionary of Philosophy and Psychology*. Robinson's article "Royce on the Origin and Development of Philosophical Terminology," has since been printed in this *Journal*, Vol. LIII (February 2, 1956), pp. 103-112.

about him, it'll shting him to the quick." Royce often told another
story about the truth. The Captain recorded in the log, "Mate
drunk today," and refused to cancel it, *because* it was true. Then
came the Mate's turn to keep the log. "Captain sober today."
The Captain stormed, but the Mate answered blandly, "It is
true, isn't it?"

Professor Daniel Robinson calls attention to the high excel-
lence of the articles by Royce in Baldwin's *Dictionary of Philosophy and Psychology,* on Greek and Latin terminology and
that of Kant and of Hegel, as well as other articles, such as the
one on the Individual. In such articles Royce escapes from his
tendency towards verboseness. He used to repeat with glee the
protest of an early reviewer, "Royce first tells us what he is
going to say, then he says it, then he says that he has said it,
and then finally he says what it was that he has said." There
were also unkind people who, after reading such sentences as "I
am, myself, in my philosophy, no mystic," started a rumor that
Royce wrote his books in German, and then let his wife translate
them. But his encyclopedia articles were almost always master-
pieces of succinct precision, in Baldwin, and in Hastings' *Encyclopedia of Religion and Ethics.* I remember his coming in one
morning to remark whimsically, "That man Hastings says he
will give me four columns in which to write all I know about
truth."

The article when it appeared was labeled, "Error and Truth,"
and ran four times that long, but far shorter than his usual
style. The article on "Negativity" suffers from being so brief
as to give little scope for his own views in his oral lectures.
That on "Monotheism" is a mere sketch of orthodox opinions,
but luckily left room for A. E. Taylor's brilliant "Theism" in a
later volume. Royce's article on "Mind" is on symbols and interpretations, and instead of the usual bibliography of the great
philosophers, has a closing note which may be summed up: "On
'Mind' read Charles Peirce." The two articles most characteristic of the later Royce are those on "Order" and "Axioms."
The latter is a masterpiece, and he was proud of it. He started
his Logic course, Philosophy 15, by assigning "Axioms," as he
began his Metaphysics, the famous Philosophy 9, by assigning
a paper on "What is Reality?" This may seem a poser, but actually a student at this stage in his development knows more
about Reality than he will ever know again.

Royce was not sympathetic with Ralph Barton Perry's advocated new ''exact'' philosophical terminology. He said Browning might have thoughts that "break through language and escape," but he had always found it possible himself to "say it in English," if you knew enough English. The inventor of a new technical term usually ends up by using it in more than one sense himself, and meanwhile nobody else is quite sure what he is talking about. It would be intolerable to have a new word for every one of the four hundred fifty or more current meanings in the Oxford Dictionary for the verb "to take." The important thing is usually not the terms used, but the way you put them together.

Harry T. Costello
Trinity College,
Hartford, Connecticut.

IV

ROYCE'S CONTRIBUTIONS TO LOGIC

What, in his own opinion, was Josiah Royce's major contribution to logic? He gave a clear answer to this question to the members of the last advanced class in logic which he taught at Harvard University during the second semester of the 1915-1916 academic year. After finishing his lectures at the end of May, he died in September. It was my privilege to complete that course in which only graduate students were enrolled, and I now especially welcome the opportunity to formulate in writing what I believe he considered his major contribution to logic.

Unfortunately much of the work Royce did in logic during the last decade of his life was never published. In a letter dated February sixth, 1942, his son, Stephen, wrote: "In the last ten years of his life he did a great deal of long and laborious work on symbolic logic, of which only a little was published because his researches were never completed." However several essays written during this period were published, especially in Hasting's *Encyclopedia of Religion and Ethics,* and the highly important "The Principles of Logic" in Ruge's *Encyclopedia of the Philosophical Sciences,* Vol. I, *Logic* (Macmillan & Co., Ltd., London, 1913). My *Royce's Logical Essays* (Wm. C. Brown, Inc., Dubuque, Iowa, 1951) is a collection of these essays. In a review of this collection, C. I. Lewis wrote: "This republication under one cover of his essays in logic and related topics is a service to those who are interested in the foremost American representative of absolute idealism or in the development of recent logical theory . . . . Perhaps we might all do well to reread these collected essays."[1]

After examining *Royce's Logical Essays,* William E. Hocking

---

[1] *Philosophy and Phenomenological Research*, Vol. XII, p. 431. The abbreviation, *RLE*, is used below for *Royce's Logical Essays* following that used by Professor Frank M. Oppenheim in his excellent "Bibliography of Royce." See his two important bibliographic notes below, Part III, p. 152.

wrote me these informative comments in a letter dated July 2, 1951: "I want to send you at once a word of thanks as well as congratulations for bringing these essays together, and throwing them into the swirl of current logical interest. They have now a good chance to be appraised both for their historical weight at the time they were published, and for elements of permanent worth.

"Royce had hopes of bringing out a work on logic. He had looked forward to the publication of Wundt's *Logik*,—for, as your book shows, he wasn't too much impressed by the view of Husserl that psychology had lost its pertinence to logic, or that Husserl himself had shaken wholly free,—and he was frankly disappointed in Wundt's production. He had not made the advance on Sigwart that Royce was hoping for. All the more, Royce wanted to have a hand in the fray. But with your work there are possiblities of seeing the total force of his thinking in this field, so that he will still 'have a hand' in it."

Students enrolled in Royce's advanced logic course were required to study the essays in Ruge's volume. Hence it served as the basic textbook for the course. In his highly competent review of this volume, C. D. Broad wrote: "The best contribution is undoubtedly Royce's. He alone deals at any length with inductive logic, and his view that induction does not involve the assumption of any law of nature but only of laws of probability, seems to me sound. The reason that he offers for the advanced state of those natural sciences that can be treated mathematically are also plausible, and it is interesting to note his suggestion that as other kinds of order systems besides that of number are worked out, we may be able to enjoy the advantages of mathematical methods in regions of investigation where quantitative considerations are impossible." [2]

Broad here gives us the clue to what Royce's major contribution to logic really is. Royce defined logic as the "Science of Order." He also stresses "the general concept of the *Orderly Array* of objects of thought, with its subordinate concepts of *Series,* of the *Correlation of Series* and of special *Order-Systems.*" And then he insists that "all these concepts are essential to the understanding of the methods thought employs in dealing with its objects." And he explains that "a general review of

---

[2] *RLE*, p. 378. Editor's note. Quoted from Broad's review in the *International Journal of Ethics*, Vol. XXIV, p. 474.

Methodology leads us to the problems of the Science of Order."[3]

In Royce's opinion this concept of *orderly array,* and its three subordinate concepts constitute the logical underpinning and structure of all of the natural sciences, both physical and biological. But, as we shall explain more fully presently, he also extends this to the social and political sciences, indeed, to all of the humanistic branches of man's knowledge by the use of his concept of *modes of action.*

That this was Royce's major contribution to logic can be substantiated by indicating how he himself connected his most technical and difficult treatise titled "The Relation of the Principles of Logic to the Foundations of Geometry" to his later essay, "The Principles of Logic." He claimed to have accomplished the following in the former treatise: "The algebra of logic, so far as I know, has not hitherto been brought into definite relation with the problem of the continuum. This is one of the things that I here accomplish. This undertaking involves proving all the principles of logic so as to make them applicable to infinite sets of entities at once. This also I have done here."[4] Thus he claims to have cancelled the distinction between geometry, hence mathematics in general, and logic, treating both as branches of a single system of principles which he named the Science of Order. It is especially noteworthy and significant that in the latter essay he specifically referred to his earlier 1905 article as proving that "the principles which are involved in any account of the nature of logical classes and their relations are capable of a restatement in terms of which we can define an extremely general order-system." And he then concludes with this prophetic affirmation: *"It at present appears to be possible to define, upon the basis of purely logical relations, and upon the basis of the aforegoing principles concerning rational activity, an order-system of entities inclusive not only of objects having the relations of the number system, but also of objects illustrating the geometrical types of order, and thus apparently including all the order-systems upon which, at least at present, the natural sciences depend for the success of their deductions."[5]* Natural sciences here obviously includes the humanistic sciences as well as the physi-

---

[3] *RLE*, p. 335.

[4] *RLE*, p. 387.

[5] *RLE*, pp. 373 and 377.

cal and biological sciences. A closer examination of Royce's concept of *modes of action* will support this conclusion.[6]

Royce begins his discussion of modes of action by asking a quite crucial question: "What order-systems must he (the logician) conceive, not as contingent and arbitrary, but as so implied in the nature of our rational activity that the effort to remove them from our world would inevitably imply their reinstatement?" The implication of this question is that any self-reflecting agent has to have open to him as options "certain possible modes of action," and it also implies that these are of such a nature that "we can apply the system of the whole numbers to characterize our own acts,"[7] even though the series of possible acts is finite and that of the whole numbers is infinite. Royce uses singing and dancing as examples of modes of action. A particular act of singing, such as a football game crowd singing the national anthem at the start of a game, is a case of such a mode of action. What Royce evidently means is that rational self-reflecting agents can perform actual overt acts that particularize the various kinds of modes of acting such as singing and dancing. He then assumes that any normal adult rational agent does in fact perform a long series of such overt particular acts during his life-span. This is always a finite series of acts that are done.

Here Royce runs into a peculiar difficulty, namely, that the modes of action are not *per se* separate particular acts, each with its own series of effects in the natural world. On the contrary each mode of acting is dyadic in the sense that it can either be done or not done, that is, one can either dance or not dance, or sing or not sing, whereas whatever act finally becomes overt and particularized in our human world at once starts a relatively long but finite series of events in that world, and these cannot be undone. Thus one set of modes of action, namely, all of the acts possible to an agent faced with a given situation where he must do something, is composed of positive and negative (yes and no) acts, either pair of which can either be done or not done. Obviously in a given suitable situation an agent can either sing or not sing, or dance or not dance. It follows that these paired

---

[6] See my discussion of "Royce's Concept of Modes of Action" in *Philosophy and Phenomenological Research*, Vol. XIV, pp. 253-257, which is reprinted in my *Crucial Issues in Philosophy* (Christopher Publishing House, Boston, Mass., 1955), from which some sentences of the following are taken.

[7] *RLE*, pp. 368 f.

modes of action are, in relation to the agent, symmetrical logical relations. But the actual overt acts any agent does sets up a series of effects in our natural world that cannot be undone, and hence its relations are non-symmetrical, logically speaking. Nevertheless, Royce contends that both sets or types of relations here involved have a well-defined logical order, and consequently the laws of logic apply to both. In my previously cited discussion of Royce's concept of modes of action, I refer to the modes of action before an act is done as a first order mode of action, and to the series following the doing of the act as a second order mode of action.

Royce's argument to prove that the laws of logic apply to both first and second order modes of action is of considerable interest. Here is his statement of the argument:

"Our modes of action are subject to the same general laws to which propositions and classes are subject. That is:

"(1)   To any 'mode of action,' such as 'to sing' or 'singing' (expressed in English either by the infinitive or by the present participle of the verb) there corresponds a mode of action, which is the *contradictory*, of the first, for example, 'not to sing' or 'not singing.' Thus, in this realm, to every x there corresponds *one*, and essentially *only* one, $\bar{x}$.

"(2)   Any pair of modes of action, such for instance as 'singing' and 'dancing,' have their 'logical product,' precisely as classes have a product, and their 'logical sum,' again, precisely as the classes possess a sum. Thus the 'mode of action' expressed by the phrase: 'To sing and to dance' is the logical product of the 'modes of action' 'to sing' and 'to dance.' The mode of action expressed by the phrase, 'Either to sing or to dance,' is the logical sum of 'to sing' and 'to dance.' These logical operations of addition and multiplication depend upon triadic relations of modes of action, precisely analogous to the triadic relation of classes. So then, to any x and $y,$ in this realm, there correspond xy and $x+y$.

"(3)   Between any two modes of action a certain dyadic, transitive and not totally non-symmetrical relation may either obtain or not obtain. This relation may be expressed by the verb 'implies.' It has precisely the same relational properties as the relation — of one class or proposition to another. Thus the mode of action expressed by the phrase, 'To sing *and* to dance,' *implies* the mode of action expressed by the phrase 'to sing.' In other words 'Singing *and* dancing,' implies 'singing.'

"(4) There is a mode of action which may be symbolized by an *o*. This mode of action may be expressed in language by the phrase, 'to do nothing,' or 'doing nothing.' There is another mode of action which may be symbolized by 1. This is the mode of action expressed in language by the phrase 'to do something,' that is, to act positively in any way whatever which involves *'not doing nothing.'* The modes of action o and 1 are contradictories each of the other.

"In consequence of these considerations, *the modes of action are a set of entities that in any case conform to the same logical laws to which classes and propositions conform.* The so-called 'Algebra of Logic' may be applied to them. A set of modes of action may therefore be viewed as a system within which the principles of logical order must be regarded as applicable."[8]

Royce is especially concerned to uncover what he called "absolute modes of activity." These are the necessary pre-suppositions of any actual moral activity whatsoever. Various names have been given to this doctrine. Royce named it "absolute pragmatism." Others have called it "activism," "universal sociology," "logic of the will," and "voluntarism." To grasp what Royce means here perhaps the best approach is to start with the quotation from Goethe's *Faust* of Mephistopheles' famous saying: *Ich bin der Geist, der stets verneint,* I am the Spirit who always denies. Here is Royce's interpretation of this notable dictum:

"If Mephistopheles always denies, his denials, which are practical as well as theoretical, are modes of action which have their place and value in a definitely limited universe of discourse, both social and ethical. In their simplest forms and instances they appear as a 'snubbing' of the proposals which others make, a sarcastic and cynical showing of contempt for human hopes and aspirations: they leave hearts desolate, ruin lives, and add to the sum of human horror. Under these circumstances, we can understand how every mode of action does indeed involve a destruction of something as well as a construction of something else, and how the not-relations involved are perfectly symmetrical, while we equally well understand why we prefer that hearts should not be made desolate, that lives should not be ruined, and that the noblest in man should not be destroyed. The world in which we condemn Mephistopheles for his negation is indeed a limited universe of discourse, but the relation between heaven

---

[8] *RLE*, pp. 374 ff.

and hell in that world is not merely a symmetrical not-relation, but an asymmetrical relation—a relation of lower and higher, of the noblest to the basest, of the heights of justice and holiness to the depths of diabolism. It is important to see that the logical symmetry of the not-relation is needed as the basis of such unsymmetrical relations between good and evil, heaven and hell, salvation and perdition. Without negation none of these contrasts could be defined, none of these distinctions between the lower and the higher could come to clear consciousness at all; hence negation is an absolutely essential function of our thought and will. Without negation there would be no clearness with regard to values, no knowledge of heaven or hell, of good or evil; hence Mephistopheles is indeed the inseparable companion of the one who is to learn what these distinctions are, and is even thereby to come into contact with what constitutes their value."[9]

In the review quoted above, C. D. Broad wrote that he thinks Royce has "failed to connect the indefinables of logic and mathematics with possible volitions." But he did not explain why Royce failed. Evidently Broad had not carefully studied the background argument in the treatise: "The Relation of the Principles of Logic to the Foundations of Geometry." It should be especially stressed that Royce's primary concern was to uncover by his acute logical analyses some of the "absolute modes of activity," and this he certainly did.

In developing this original theory of types of order-systems and modes of action Royce was neither a conceptualist nor a nominalist. He was a realist. To him order-systems are objectively real. It is true that rational beings create many such order-systems. But it is also true that such beings discover many order-systems that are completely independent. The cosmos, the entire universe is through and through intelligible because serial order-systems, united by logical relations, both symmetrical and non-symmetrical, constitute reality. Royce's insistence that intelligible mathematical and logical order-systems are both created and discovered by self reflecting thinkers perforce demands that they be pronounced objectively real. He admitted that it is impossible for any rational being to define exactly "the totality of all possible modes of action," and that it is also impossible for such a being to comprehend the entire

---

[9] *RLE*, pp. 199 f.

collection of objective order-systems. Royce says that the Theory of Assemblages shows this "to involve logical contradiction."

Perhaps the best way to comprehend his logical realism is to interpret his concept of a standard self-reflecting mind that is capable of creating objectively real order-systems that possess what he calls "logical reality." Here he is under the influence of Kant's theory of any rational being and his possible experience, but he modified the Kantian theory by basing the hypothetical rationality of such a being on the activity of willing rather than on the passivity of sensing. Royce insists that logical realism is a necessary presupposition of rational activity wherever it exists or is assumed to exist. "To deny this is to abandon the very conception of rational activity," he wrote. In case there is even one rational being who can conceive what order-systems are in their logical structure then such systems are *ipso facto* real. This standard rational being need not be human. Nor is Royce assuming that such a standard rational mind would be a solipsist. This would contradict his logical realism. Individual minds are essential when an order-system is discovered, but the order-system is objectively real whether it is known by any rational being or not. Let us use one of Royce's own illustrations to make this clear. In a letter dated July 19, 1951, his son, Stephen, wrote that his father told him that the difficulty he was having in finding a unit of measure for harmonic construction was "much like that which would be expressed by a highly intelligent jellyfish for whom space relations are suffering constant and irregular change from moment to moment of his existence." If the jellyfish could reflect, if it had a rational self-reflecting mind, the order-system constituted by its movements in the ocean which is objectively real, could be known by it, albeit with great difficulty. Royce's primary concern was to uncover by logical analysis the actual framework of order-systems of all types—a framework he claims possessed "logical reality." Undoubtedly one must deduce from his theory that the orderliness of the space relations involved in the moment to moment gyrations of the total existence of any particular jellyfish in the ocean constitutes an objective-order system. This must be an implication of his logical realism, and perhaps this extreme and trivial example may help to clarify this implication.

Royce was a master dialectician. It scarcely needs mentioning that he had a comprehensive knowledge and a profound understanding of the whole development of dialectics from Zeno and his paradoxes through Plato, Aristotle, and the Stoics. His four special articles in Baldwin's *Dictionary of Philosophy and Psychology* show how extensive his grasp of dialectics was. They are entitled "Greek Terminology," "Kant's Terminology," "Hegel's Terminology," and "Latin and Scholastic Terminology."[10] Anyone reading almost any of his writings will at once recognize that he was adept in the use of the dialectical method. The question now emerges: What contribution to logic did Royce make that grew out of his understanding of dialectics and adds significantly to that subject?

The clue to an answer to this question is found in his meaningful distinction between a superficial and a profound interpretation of the meaning of Hegel's famous thesis, antithesis, and synthesis form of the dialectical method. According to Royce, Hegel's superficial use of this method consists of showing that common sense ideas of the man in the street are so vague as to be virtually meaningless. Like Socrates Hegel used his dialectical method to call such ideas in question and hence this is essentially a negative use of the method that awakens a sceptical attitude. In sharp contrast to this negative use Hegel's profound employment of the dialectical method was positive and constructive. It establishes the fact that any really valid idea or judgment is one that is identical with the objective order-system it seeks to uncover and make clear. Interpreting Hegel, Royce writes: "the fully grown *Begriff* is itself the object sought, the curtain is the picture, and the thought is the being."

On the other hand, Royce recognized the importance of the new triadic theory of knowledge developed by his friend and colleague, Charles Sanders Peirce. In Volume II of his *The Problem of Christianity,* he devoted several chapters to an exposition and clarification of this theory, claiming that it grew out of his friend's analysis of logical comparison. In his early logical writing Peirce proved that a third term or mediator is required in all comparisons whether they be mathematical, or literary, or social and historical. This is the source of his conception of interpretation as a triadic theory of knowledge on which Royce placed so much emphasis in his essay entitled "Mind" as well as in *The Problem of Christianity.* Briefly

---

[10] See my article discussing these articles in the *Journal of Philosophy*, Vol. LIII, pp. 103-112, reprinted above.

stated this theory claims that interpretation which requires the triadic relation between an interpreter, a sign or symbol which he interprets, and another rational being to whom he interprets this sign is the final, ultimate form of human knowledge. It is also a genuine synthesis of sense knowledge and of conceptual knowledge. Note that two implicit meanings are embodied in these two sentences, that of Peirce—*interpreter, sign* and *intelligent recipient* of the interpretation, and that of Hegel, interpretation as the *synthesis* of the *thesis*—perceptual knowledge, and the *antithesis*—conceptual knowledge.

Perceptual and conceptual knowledge are primarily solipsistic in the sense that in each an individual thinker is the implied knower. This means that the cognitive relation in each case is dyadic. Think, for example, of Aristotle's well-known sayings: We sense that we sense," and "we understand that we understand." Obviously the first saying refers to sense knowledge and second to conceptual knowledge. Surely his conclusion "we know that we exist'' would be what Peirce called knowledge by interpretation, since it implies communication with other knowers, as Aristotle recognized.

Royce knew that Peirce did not reach this new conception of knowledge by interpretation as a result of his study of Hegel. He says Peirce was not under the influence of Hegel when he first formulated his theory in writing, and that his illustrations are drawn from mathematics, whereas those of Hegel were ethical and historical. Nevertheless Royce recognized that there is *no essential inconsistency between the profound meaning of the Hegelian dialectical method and Peirce's theory of interpretation*. His own contribution to the development of the triadic theory of knowledge by interpretation is his bringing the Hegelian theory under the Peirce theory as a special case. This he succinctly states: "Peirce's concept of interpretation defines an extremely general process of which the Hegelian dialectical triadic process is a very special case."[11] What other logician but Royce knew the Peirce and Hegelian theories well enough to pass such a judgment? His contribution was that of combining the truth of Peirce's theory of interpretation with the deeper meaning of the dialectical method of Hegel.

Royce also pointed out the superiority of this broad form of

[11] *The Problem of Christianity*, Vol. II, (Macmillan Co., N. Y., 1913), p. 185.

the theory of knowledge as interpretation over the theory developed by Bertrand Russell in the *Principles of Mathematics*. Of special importance in this connection is a recent statement about what Royce said in a course in logic taught by Russell at Harvard University in the spring semester of 1914, when he gave some introductory lectures prior to Russell's late arrival to take over the course. Professor Victor F. Lenzen, who was recording secretary of this class, writes: "He (Royce) contrasted the theories of Russell and Peirce. Professor Royce explained that Russell's theory, in which mind and object were related by a dyadic relation, was a dyadic theory of knowledge, whereas Peirce's theory, which involved the conception of interpretation, was a triadic theory. Royce agreed with Peirce that the process of cognition was a social one."[12]

Thus Royce used Peirce's conception of a community of interpretation to expand into its final form his earlier theory that knowledge is social and purposive. This is also the fullest fruition of the profound form of Hegel's dialectical method. Important as sense knowledge and conceptual knowledge are, when considered separately, they become far more significant when they are synthesized into interpretative knowledge shared by competent communicators. This is the logical significance of Royce's concept of the great community, which he developed in the last book he wrote which bears the title: *The Hope of the Great Community*, (1916).

This interpretative and purposive conception of knowledge is to be found in germ in one of Royce's earliest essays entitled "On Purpose in Thought." It was written in 1880, but it was first published in *Fugitive Essays*, (1920), edited by J. Loewenberg. In this essay he defended the thesis that the purpose of thought is to seek and find truth, or, in his own words, "the attainment of truth is the end of thought." But he there rejected the correspondence theory of the nature of truth, in an argument

---

[12] *Transactions of the Charles S. Peirce Society*, Vol. I, p. 4 (1965). On Royce's relation to Peirce see H. N. Lee: "Royce as a Logician" in *Tulane Studies in Philosophy*, Vol. IV, (New Orleans, La., 1955), pp. 61-75. Professor Lee also calls attention to the importance of Royce's "Supplementary Essay" to *The World and the Individual*, with its original concept of a "self-representative system." "This argument," he writes, "is almost altogether an argument from the then relatively new mathematical theory of infinite numbers." He quotes Morris R. Cohen's statement: "The realistic argument as to the nature of mathematics was first advanced by Royce in the two volumes of *The World and the Individual*" (p. 67). Cohen cites Vol. I, p. 256.

very much like the one he used in his "Error and Truth" article in Hasting's *Encyclopedia of Religion and Ethics* which was written in 1912. He formulated the correspondence theory in these words: "Truth is the agreement between our thought and the reality which is independent of it." Royce says that such a conception could only be supported by subjective evidence. This would finally end in the view that "some thought which we have and know well corresponds in an entirely unknown way with a reality of which directly we know simply nothing." In the end the asserted correspondence of thought with reality turns out to be merely the thinker's own inner conviction that his thoughts are in harmony with reality.

When we treat this conviction as an axiomatic certainty, and claim that thought rests upon basic axioms that are self-evident truths, we can define the end of thought as "finding and stating axioms," and "bringing all our beliefs into harmony and connection with the axioms." Then we would have to show that all non-axiomatic statements are in agreement with and follow from the axioms. Nevertheless, Royce here and elsewhere rejects self-evidence. Frequently he warned his advanced logic students that self-evidence is a dangerous principle in mathematics as well as in logic. In his essay "The Principles of Logic" he wrote: "In all the older attempts to characterize the mathematical systems of an orderly type, great stress was laid upon the assumption of so-called 'self-evident' *Axioms*. The example of Euclid in his geometry, and the Aristotelian logical theory regarding the necessity of founding all proof upon 'immediate' certainties,— these were the paramount influences in determining this tendency. But the more the logician considers the so-called 'self-evident' principles of the older mathematical statements, the more reason does he see to condemn self-evidence as in itself a fitting logical guide. *When we call an assertion self-evident we generally do so because we have not yet sufficiently considered the complexity of the relations involved.* And many propositions have been supposed to be self-evident truths that upon closer acquaintance have turned out to be decidedly inexact in their meaning, or altogether incorrect."[13]

Although Royce named his own theory "absolute pragmatism," nevertheless, he rejected the pragmatist theory of truth of his friend and colleague, William James, as well as the instrumenta-

---

[13] *RLE*, p. 369.

list form of this theory originated and defended by John Dewey. In the article "Error and Truth" referred to above, he subjected this general theory to sharp critical examination. Although admitting its partial truth, he proved conclusively, with telling examples, that there is a kind of truth whose very nature contradicts the pragmatist's definition of truth as being what works or what is instrumental in guiding the thinker to new knowledge. He also proved with equal finality that pragmatism itself rests upon a proposition that cannot possibly be tested pragmatically, and he clearly states that proposition. Hence, to quote his own words, "there is a sort of truth of which Pragmatism gives no account." To be sure, this Roycean argument can be and has been ignored by advocates of the pragmatist theory. But they have never refuted it. In fact, it is irrefutable.

Royce's own theory of truth has been classified as a form of the classic coherence theory. To him some laws of logic are self-substantiating, and they are mutually consistent. These are the foundation of all thought and action. They are discovered by a logical and constructive analysis of highly complicated experiences, whether these are considered at the level of ordinary, macroscopic common sense experience, or at the level of technical microscopic scientific experience, that is to say, whether the thinker is analyzing chairs and tables or atoms, neutrons and electrons. Royce always insisted that a true proposition is presupposed and necessarily used in every attempt to deny it. He stated this principle clearly and italicised it in the essay "The Principles of Logic," and also elsewhere in his writings. He wrote: *"In brief, whatever actions are such, whatever types of actions are such, whatever results of activity, whatever conceptual constructions are such, that the very act of getting rid of them, or of thinking them away, logically implies their presence are known to us indeed both empirically and pragmatically (since we note their presence and learn of them through action); but they are also absolute. And any account which succeeds in telling what they are has absolute truth. Such truth is a 'construction' or 'creation' for activity determines its nature. It is 'found', for we observe it when we act."*[14] Thus there is, according to Royce a system of self-substantiating and coherent logical principles upon which the entire system of knowledge and action rests. Whatever propositions are true in any of the

---

[14] *RLE*, p. 365.

exact sciences, indeed, in any of the many branches of human knowledge, are true because of their coherence and consistency with these self-substantiating logical laws.

The contributions to logic of the kind of an intellectual genius Royce was are not confined to the doctrines, theories, and ideas which he originated or enriched. He awakened the spirit of logical inquiry in his most gifted students. For over a third of a century he was on active duty as a teacher of advanced seminars and courses in scientific method, logic, metaphysics, ethics, and the history of philosophy at Harvard University. Royce had what one of his most gifted students, J. Loewenberg, has aptly characterized as a "Synoptic Vision," and he awakened this same capacity in such students. He liked least those students who, parrot-like, merely thought their teacher's thoughts and gave them back to him in required written reports. He liked most and best those students who differed from him and gave what they thought were valid reasons for their own interpretation. In his Preface to the American edition of Gabriel Marcel's *Royce's Metaphysics,* W. E. Hocking, another of his most gifted students, tells of an experience he had when he turned in an essay in one of Royce's seminars, which contained a passage rather sharply dissenting from a position taken by Royce. Hocking writes: "I was expecting a radical criticism from my revered professor. Instead, when Royce handed my essay back, he pointed out the dissenting passage with the comment, 'This is your insight: You must adhere to that!' Without assenting to my own view, he had given me his blessing for its development." This, then, indicates what the spirit of Royce was as a teacher of logic.

Appended are the names and the titles of some books written by logicians who studied under Royce:

Cohen, Morris R. (1880-1947) wrote *Reason and Nature: An Essay on the Meaning of Scientific Method* (Kegan Paul, Trench Co., London, 1931.) Cohen also co-authored with Ernest Nagel a college logic textbook titled *An Introduction to Logic and Scientific Method,* and wrote *A Preface to Logic,* 1944. He contributed to *Papers in Honor of Josiah Royce on his Sixtieth Birthday* (1916), an important essay: "Neo-Realism and the Philosophy of Royce."

Costello, Harry Todd (1885-1960) was chosen by Royce as recorder for his Seminar for the academic year 1913-14. His notebooks as recorder have been edited by Gordon Smith and published under the title, *Josiah Royce's Seminar, 1913-14,* with an essay, "Process and Analysis in the Philosophy of Royce" by Richard Hocking (Rutgers University Press, 1963).[15]

Ducasse, Curt John (1881-   ) wrote *Causation and the Types of Necessity* (University of Washington Press, 1924). He served for one year as president of the American Association for Symbolic Logic.

Eaton, Ralph Monroe (1894-1932) wrote *Symbolism and Truth, An Introduction to the Theory of Knowledge* (Harvard University Press, 1925, reprinted 1964, Dover Publications, New York) and *General Logic, An Introductory Survey* (Charles Scribner's Sons, N. Y., 1931).

Lewis, Clarence Irving (1883-1964) authored *A Survey of Symbolic Logic* (University of California Press, Berkeley, 1918), co-authored with C. R. Langford, a textbook entitled *Symbolic Logic* (Century Co., 1932), and wrote *Analysis of Knowledge*

---

[15] This book honors both Royce and Costello. The full title of Richard Hocking's essay is "Process and Analysis in the Philosophy of Royce," and it justly appraises the renewal of interest in his thought. The *appendix* reprints Costello's centenary address, "Recollections of Royce's Seminar on Comparative Methodology," and contains a complete bibliography of Costello's writings.

Costello served as secretary of Royce's Seminar in Logic for the academic year, 1913-1914. Among participants in this Seminar were distinguished staff members of Harvard University: L. J. Henderson, E. E. Southard, F. A. Woods, R. F. A. Hoernlé, and nine graduate students, some of whom later won high distinction, including A. P. Brogan, T. S. Eliot, R. M. Blake, L. T. Troland, and N. N. Sen Gupta. Costello kept two notebooks. In one he recorded, almost *verbatim*, what Royce and others said during each session. In the other he wrote a summary of each session, presumably to be read at the opening of the next session. These notebooks are now in the Trinity College Library.

This book consists chiefly of their contents arranged for each session in two parts, one entitled *Notes*, and the other, *Summary*. Since the *Notes* were written during each session, and the *Summaries* after Seminar adjourned, the two are quite different in both form and content. The *Notes* are in dialogue form. Some of the statements are most important and others are quite trivial. The editor faced a dilemma. If he deleted what he deemed trivia, he might omit something others would consider essential to the argument, but if he included everything, he would have somewhat of a hodgepodge that would confuse the reader. He chose the second horn.

The *Summaries* contain Costello's considered evaluations of the argument that went on in each session, and often include his strong critical reactions to opinions expressed, as well as his own position. Hence the *Summaries* are all highly important. If the student can and will winnow the wheat from the chaff in the *Notes*, and use this to enrich the *Summaries*, he will be well rewarded.

and Valuation (Open Court Publishing Co., 1946).[16] Lewis taught logic at Harvard University for nearly forty years.

Scheffer, Henry Maurice (1883-1964) taught advanced courses in logic at Harvard University for thirty-six years. He published only monographs, but an important volume of essays in his honor was edited by Paul Henle, and titled *Structure, Method, and Meaning* (Liberal Arts Press, N. Y., 1951).

Wiener, Norbert (1894-1964) was a mathematical prodigy, receiving his Ph. D. degree from Harvard University at the exceptionally early age of under nineteen. In his autobiography, *Ex-Prodigy, My Childhood and Youth* (Simon & Shuster, N. Y.) Wiener refers to Royce as a "brilliant" and "many-sided man." He said that he attended Royce's Seminar in Scientific Method for two years, and commented "it gave me some of the most valuable training I ever had" (p. 164). He taught mathematics at Massachusetts Institute of Technology and wrote *Cybernetics* (John Wiley & Sons, Inc., N. Y., 1948) and numerous mathematical treatises and articles. He helped lay the foundation for the recent rapidly developing computer science and industrial automation.

The continuous stream of time sweeps into oblivion all ordinary people, and even many who are superior persons. But Royce was not an ordinary nor just a superior logician. He was a logical genius and the teacher of geniuses. Whoever in future centuries is able to write a competent history of the development of modern logic, during the more than a century he and his students have labored, will perforce be required to allot a generous space to the recording of their achievements and the interpreting of their original contributions to the Science of Order.[17]

---

[16] For comments of Lewis on Royce see the *Philosophical Review*, Vol. XXV, pp. 407-419, republished in *Papers in Honor of Josiah Royce on his Sixtieth Birthday* (New York, 1916), and his *Survey of Symbolic Logic* (Berkeley, California, 1918), pp. 362-367. On Lewis see Donald Williams in *Philosophy and Phenomenological Research*, Vol. XXVI, pp. 159-172, "Clarence Irving Lewis, 1883-1964," and the *Commemorative Symposium on C. I. Lewis* in the *Journal of Philosophy*, Vol. LXI, No. 19, 1964.

[17] Reprinted from *Revue Internationale de Philosophie*, Numbers 79-80, 1967, fascicule 1-2, pp. 60-76.

V

ROYCE'S CONCEPTION OF GOD

In 1895 a notable symposium was held at the Philosophical Union of the University of California (Berkeley). The participants were Professors Josiah Royce (1855-1916), Joseph Le Conte (1823-1901), G. H. Howison (1834-1917), and Sidney E. Mezes (1863-1931); and the general theme under consideration was *The Conception of God*. When the book containing the original contributions of these distinguished philosophers was published in 1897 it bore the subtitle, "A philosophical discussion concerning the nature of the divine idea as a demonstrable reality," and it also included a long supplementary essay by Professor Royce entitled, "The Absolute and the Individual," in which he amplified his position and replied to his critics. The importance of this supplementary essay is indicated by the fact that it restates the author's earlier argument of *The Religious Aspects of Philosophy*, and contains the germs of his well-known Gifford Lectures, *The World and the Individual* (2 vols., 1901), as well as that of his significant later works, *The Philosophy of Loyalty* (1908), *The Sources of Religious Insight* (1912), and *The Problems of Christianity* (2 vols., 1913). See also his article entitled "Monotheism" in Hastings's *Encylopedia of Religion and Ethics*.

An introduction by Professor Howison, who was also the editor of the book, not only contains an excellent summary of the discussions, but succinctly states the status of the philosophy of religion at the end of the nineteenth century. He pointed out that attempts to establish religion on a rational foundation had been on the defensive during the last half of the century as a result of the influence of the doctrines of the Unconditioned of Sir William Hamilton, and of the Unknowable of Herbert Spencer, and of the atheistic positivism of Auguste Comte. All of these doctrines were strongly reinforced by Darwin's proofs of biological evolution. Their popularity made necessary a reconstruction of theological conceptions to bring them into accord with the new ideas of evolution. This reconstruction took the form of the doctrine of an Immanent God. Although it was definitely built upon Kantian and Hegelian foundations, this doctrine was quite original and thoroughly modern. Hence it became the chief reliance of those thinkers who refused to surrender to those agnosticisms that were based upon the theory of evolution. Now the significant fact is that this idealistic philosophy of religion was dominant among most Protestant groups at the end of the nineteenth century. Under the leadership of John Fiske evolutionism and idealism united in spreading the doctrine that there exists one and only one Immanent Spirit.

All the contributors to the symposium at Berkeley accepted a personal God as real, and they were all united in holding that there is a close correlation among three basic concepts that are common to philosophy and religion, namely, God, freedom, and immortality. In his introduction Howison explains that all the participants agree that neither of these three concepts can be properly interpreted without using statements of each of the other two. Quoting his own words: *"No God except with human Selves free and immortal in some sense, in some degree or other;* and so, likewise, *mutatis mutandis,* of Freedom and of Immortality."* (p. xiv) Now it must be admitted that this is an extensive and significant agreement, and that it is sufficient to justify the inclusion of all of these philosophers under the common name of idealists. Moreover, some other prominent thinkers of that period, who were not participants in this famous symposium, are correctly classified as idealists. These include especially Borden Parker Bowne (1847-1910), a first-rate thinker and founder of personalism in the United States, and William Torrey Harris (1835-1909), leading representative of the Hegelian St. Louis School of Philosophy, and U. S. Commissioner of Education. We are therefore, justified in concluding that idealism dominated the thinking of the majority of leading philosophers who contributed to the philosophy of religion in the United States at the dawn of the twentieth century.

Nevertheless, there were profound differences among these philosophers with respect to their interpretations of the meaning of the three basic concepts—God, Freedom, and Immortality, and these differences came to sharp expression in the symposium. Royce defended a doctrine of *monistic and absolutistic personalism.* Here is his succinct statement of this doctrine: "The Divine Will is simply *that aspect of the Absolute which is*

*expressed in the concrete and differentiated individuality of the
world.* Hereby the world appears, not as a barely abstract
world of pure ideas, but as a world of manifested individuals,
known in the unity of the one transcendent moment of the Absolute Experience, but there known as a discrete and clearly
contrasted collection of beings, whose presence everywhere expresses, amid all the wealth of meaning which the whole em-
bodies, an element of transcendent Freedom." (pp. 202 f.)

Howison advocated *pluralistic personalism.* He sharply criti-
cized Royce for merging individual persons in a single rational
and free World-Will, and insisted that his argument contains a
mystical and an antiethical tendency. Accordingly, Howison
clearly formulates his own conception in this excellent statement:
". . . the human consciousness is seen to have, in its total unity,
the all-encompassing form of a CONSCIENCE—that Complete
Reason, of a truly infinite sphere, in which the primal self-consciousness of the creature *actively* posits the Ideal which is its
real world of being. In this complete reason, or Conscience, the
single spirit sees itself as indeed a *person*—a self-active member
of a manifold *system* of persons, all alike self-active in the inclusive unit of their being: all independent *centres of origina-
tion,* so far as *efficient* causation is concerned; all moving from
"within," i.e., each from its own *thought,* and harmonized in a
society of accordant free-agents, not by any efficient causation,
but by the operation of what has been called, since Aristotle,
final causation—the attraction of an Ideal Vision, the vision of
that CITY OF GOD which they constitute, and in which, recipro-
cally, they have their being. . . ." (pp. 91 f.)

Le Conte upheld a special form of pluralism which is called
evolutional idealism. This he clearly stated in a summary of his
position: "I assume, then, the immanence of Deity in Nature.
Furthermore, . . . I regard *physical* and *chemical* forces, or the
forces of dead Nature, as a portion of the omnipresent Divine
Energy in a *diffused, unindividuated state,* and therefore *not-
self-active* but having its phenomena determined directly by the
Divine Energy. Individuation of this Energy, i.e., self-activity,
begins, as I suppose, with Life, and proceeds, *pari passu* with
organization of matter, to complete itself as a Moral Person in
man. . . . On this view, spirit—which is a spark of Divine Energy—is a potential in dead Nature, a germ in plants, a
quickened embryo in animals, and comes to birth into a higher
world of spirit-life in man. Self consciousness—from which

flows all that is distinctive of man—is the sign of birth into the spiritual world. Thus an effluence from the Divine Person flows downward into Nature to rise again by evolution to recognition of, and communion with, its own Source." (pp. 76 f.)

The twentieth century opened with idealistic philosophy of religion dominant in the United States. But it had a triune form. One group of philosophers followed Royce's absolutistic personalism, another followed the pluralistic personalism of Howison, and another followed the evolutional idealism of Le Conte. Today, as we approach the seventh decade of the twentieth century, each of these three forms of idealistic philosophy of religion is still vigorously advocated.

In the *Varieties of Religious Experience,* William James' purpose was to seek and to discover "the unique nature of religious experience which is ultimately conclusive in respect to the judgment as to what religion in general is." To accomplish this purpose he selected from a rich store of autobiographical and first-hand reports of religious people those that were most unique and original, and he classified these into types. He called this the empirical method to differentiate it from the rationalistic method of idealists. In using the word empirical he was not altogether clear since he also spoke of an empirical philosophy as well as an empirical psychological method. This empirical philosophy was his version of *pragmatism.* Undoubtedly, he meant that the study of religion should be confined to the analysis of inner religious experience of those individuals who are deeply religious. Accordingly, he used numerous pious persons to discover the different types of individual religious experience, dealing specially with conversion and counter-conversion, prayer and meditation, and the contrast between the religion of the healthy-minded and that of those he called sick souls.

Obviously a major defect in such a method is its neglect of the religious community which results from its exclusive emphasis upon the inner religious life of devout individuals. Royce pointed this out in the preface of his *Problems of Christianity,* and especially emphasized the fact that his own method stood in sharp contrast to that of James on this important issue. This contrast between the religious experience of individuals and social religious experience as exemplified in the Church is crucial for a philosophy of religion. Royce wrote: "James supposed that the religious experience of a church must needs be 'conventional,' and consequently must be lacking in depth and in sincerity.

This, to my mind, was a profound and momentous error in the whole religious philosophy of our greatest American master in the study of the psychology of religious experience. All experience must be *at least* individual experience; but unless it is *also social* experience, and unless the whole religious community which is in question unites to share it, this experience is but as sounding brass, and as a tinkling cymbal." (Vol. I, p. xv) On this point Royce is unquestionably right.

VI

HOCKING AND MARCEL ON ROYCE'S METAPHYSICS

Although Josiah Royce rejected the pragmatic philosophy of William James and the instrumentalism of John Dewey, he did name his own position absolute pragmatism, because he was essentially committed to the belief that men can make durable contributions to reality and always do so when they put themselves in accord with that creative Absolute in whom they live and move and have their being. Here it is not my intention to expound Royce's absolute pragmatism in any detail, but I will undertake to sketch one extremely significant step forward in the interpretation of his philosophy that has been made by two of his most penetrating, sympathetic, and understanding interpreters—Professor William E. Hocking and Dr. Gabriel Marcel, French Catholic theistic existentialist philosopher. Like Royce, both of these philosophers have been Gifford Lecturers in England, they are recognized first class thinkers, and each has added something distinctive to Royce's metaphysics.

In his searching essay entitled "Marcel and the Ground Issues of Metaphysics" Hocking called attention to Marcel's early work on Royce's metaphysics in these words: "During 1918-19 he (Marcel) had published four articles which to this date, so far as I know, constitute the best monograph on Royce's metaphysical thought. This was issued in 1945 as a single volume which should by all means be translated into English." Acting on this suggestion I persuaded one of my graduate students of the University of Southern California, Mrs. Virginia Ringer and her husband, Mr. Gordon Ringer, to translate Dr. Gabriel Marcel's *Royce's Metaphysics,* and their translation was published by Henry Regnery Company in 1956. We had the good fortune to obtain a special introduction to the English edition from Gabriel Marcel, and a prefatory statement from Professor Hocking. These two statements, together with the original (1918-19) exposition of Royce's metaphysics are now available for students

71

of Royce, and they throw a good deal of light on some aspects of his metaphysics.

In his prefatory statement, Hocking calls attention to the two inseparable aspects of Royce's philosophy, "the boldly imaginative scheme of metaphysical idealism" which was designated above "absolute pragmatism," and his careful analysis of the "logical and mathematical texture of things." He then reaffirms what he had previously written: "I have long hoped for the publication in English of this, the first, and still in my judgment the most substantial and prescient discussion of Royce's entire metaphysical outlook." And he especially mentions the fact that Gabriel Marcel "has dealt with the scrupulous technical conscience of Royce from the standpoint of an equally scrupulous technical conscience," and "reached his important judgments of Royce, affirmative and critical, on the basis of an illuminating analysis" of Royce's writings.

Hocking's now classic work entitled *The Meaning of God in Human Experience* elaborates and expounds in intricate detail his major insight that took him beyond Royce, namely, that *feeling is cognitive.*

Marcel's *Foreword* to the English edition of *Royce's Metaphysics* confirms and accepts this advance Hocking made beyond Royce. He begins by quoting from his *Metaphysical Journal* under the date of August 23, 1918. He writes: "I was talking about judgments involving 'I,' such as 'I am tired' and I observed that 'there is a pure and simple feeling,' that is to say an absolute, or something which imitates an absolute, something not related to something else or mediatised. In the judgment of the 'I' it is precisely the non-relation which functions as the *him* or *it;* on this non-relation the feeling, now become a predicate, depends. . . . Yet this 'I' seems always to be posited as being in confrontation with a *thou* for whom in turn I myself am a *thou;* and it is in function of this dialogue and in relation to it that a *he* or *it* can be defined, that is, an independent world or at least that is—doubtless by a fiction—treated as independent. Here lies the profound importance of Royce's triadism and I think it has never been made sufficiently explicit. In more intelligible language, all independent reality can and must be treated as a *third party.* And if a *third party* supposes a dialogue it is nevertheless true to say that all dialogue is given to itself as a *third party.*" I show immediately afterward in a non-Roycean sense, how "a sort of slow transition from pure dialectics to love," can be realized "in the measure in which the *thou* becomes *thou* more and more profoundly." "If my memory is exact, there is nothing in Royce which corresponds to this phenomenological analysis."

In this notable passage Marcel shows already that he was interpreting Royce in terms of Hocking's insight. This, he himself, at once confirms in this statement: "I am certain, however, that several years before I began to study Royce, I had read . . . the *magnum opus* of W. E. Hocking, *The Meaning of God in Human Experience* which, I am sure, had a lasting influence on me. But it cannot be doubted that Hocking's book was an advance on Royce's thought, an advance in the direction of that metaphysical realism toward which I resolutely tended.

"Had these encounters succeeded one another in logical order, I should have read Royce before reading Hocking. But such was not the case."

Hocking points out that Marcel's French phrase "un tiers" is mistranslated as "a third party" instead of simply "a third" or "a third entity" (in a dialogue), and adds "to treat such independent reality as a 'third party' spoils the 'dialogue' and misses what I take to be Royce's sense." And what was it that Royce meant? Obviously he thought that minds communicate with each other by interpreting the same sign or third entity and not directly, whereas both Marcel and Hocking argue for a direct intersubjective communication. Both of these thinkers rejected the double translation theory of how one mind knows another. This double translation theory, as stated by Hocking, assumes "that all communications from A to B must be by way of two translations: first, from A's thoughts into physical signs capable of affecting B's sense receptors and thus his brain; and second, from this brain-effect into B's thoughts. Two translations, two chances of error, of course, but also one—extremely important—chance for control,—whether for reserve, or for calculated order of utterance, or for deception and the whole bevy of moral issues there appending." Hocking states quite clearly exactly how he and Marcel are in agreement, both negatively and positively, on this theory of a direct intersubjective communication. He writes: "It was in this general area that Marcel's enquiries and mine had been independently working; and it is not surprising that with whatever differences in problem-setting, and in the experiences that for us were severely decisive, our results converged. First of all in the negative judgment that the double-translation theory of meaning-to-meaning solely *via* the blind gate of sensation is inadequate; and then in the affirmative judgment that something like a direct participation of mind in mind is a primary datum of experience." (P.451)

Although both Hocking and Marcel built their metaphysics on the foundation that was laid by Royce, and although both were in agreement on the necessity of going beyond his triadic theory of interpretation to their conception of intersubjective communication nevertheless, it seems clear to me that Hocking is nearer to Royce's absolutism than is Marcel. But it must be admitted that in his article entitled "Marcel and the Ground Issues of Metaphysics," Hocking separates Marcel from Kirkegaard and other existentialists on the ground that he discovers an identity between being and value whereas they do not. In this essay Hocking also restates his own position on the problem of evil so as to bring it into closer accord with that of Marcel. Consequently, my conclusion is that both men are Royceans, veering in the direction of contemporary theistic existentialism, with Hocking somewhat more friendly to absolutism than Marcel.

I am appending here my review of the English translation of Gabriel Marcel's *Royce's Metaphysics,* which appeared in *Philosophy and Phenomenological Research,* Vol. XVIII No. I, September, 1957, pp. 115 f.

Royce's Metaphysics. Gabriel Marcel. Translated by Virginia and Gordon Ringer, with a Preface by W. E. Hocking and an Author's Foreword to the English Edition. Chicago: Henry Regnery Company, 1956. Pp. xii, 180.

In his Preface, Professor Hocking writes: "I have long hoped for the publication in English of this, and still in my judgment the most substantial and prescient of Royce's entire metaphysical outlook." (P. vi) Certainly the value of the English edition is much enhanced by Professor Hocking's own comments on Royce's personality, and by the author's explanation of what induced him "during the First World War, to undertake a comprehensive study of Royce's thought." (P. ix.) After writing this study based on a careful analysis of Royce's writings, especially the two series of Gifford Lectures, Gabriel Marcel himself became a Gifford lecturer. Hence we have here a study of the profound metaphysics of the ablest representative of Absolute Idealism in America by the most distinguished living theistic existentialist. It follows that this book is a must for every up-to-date philosophical library.

This book is divided into two parts. Part One is entitled "Royce's Metaphysical System." It consists of eight chapters, the titles of which are: I. The Problem of the Relation Between the Idea and the Object; II. The Fourth Conception of Being; III. The Nature of Individuality; IV. The One and the Many; V. Freedom and the Problem of Evil; VI. Time and Eternity; VII. The Transition to the Theory of Nature; and VIII. The World of Description and the World of Appreciation. Anyone at all acquainted with Royce's writings will at once recognize how central each of these titles is.

Part Two deals with "Royce's Later Philosophy" in three chapters: IX. The Theory of Loyalty; X. The Theory or Interpretation; and XI. The Philosophy of Christianity.

To the reviewer, this treatise indicates that Marcel leans more towards the spiritual pluralism of such thinkers as Bowne, Howison, and Ward than he does towards the Absolute Idealism of Royce. Nevertheless, his understanding of Royce is profound, and his indebtedness to him is quite obvious and freely acknowledged. Some light is thrown on the relation of Marcel to Hocking in the Preface and Foreword, but on this relationship, which both thinkers acknowledge to be close, see Professor Hocking's significant article entitled "Marcel and the Ground Issues of Metaphysics" in *Philosophy and Phenomenological Research,* Vol. XIV, pp. 439ff.

PART TWO

ESSAYS ON THE PHILOSOPHY OF

WILLIAM ERNEST HOCKING

VII

WILLIAM ERNEST HOCKING

August 10, 1873—June 12, 1966

From among my numerous memories of William Ernest Hocking, my distinguished professor, esteemed colleague, and cherished friend there comes to mind a statement of his, originally prepared in honor of his own revered teacher, Josiah Royce. The occasion for this statement was Professor Jacob Loewenberg's "Royce's Synoptic Vision," which was written for the observance of the centenary of Josiah Royce's birth and first delivered in March, 1955, at Boston University. Hocking attended, and he wrote me that the lecture was a good one. Arrangements were made for Loewenberg to repeat this lecture in Royce Hall on the Campus of the University of California at Los Angeles on July 31st. When I was asked to serve as master of ceremonies, I invited Hocking to send a suitable statement to be read at this meeting. My letter was forwarded to him at the Phillips House of the Massachusetts General Hospital where he was convalescing from a knee injury. He graciously responded with a statement in his own handwriting which was read at this meeting. It is such a precious gem in his unique style that it seems appropriate to reproduce it here. He entitled it "On the Centenary Year of Royce's Birth."

"Great art requires two qualities: a true perception of the enduring meaning of common things, and an incorruptible veracity of reporting that meaning. Great philosophy requires these two and one more: besides the vision and the veracity of the artist, philosophy requires the indomitable pursuit of consistency among all the visions within a single conspectus of the whole.

"The artist and the prophet are justified in living by intuition, reporting their perceptions one by one—not with contempt for consistency, but in the faith that what growing experience reveals will in time reveal also its own coherence. But philosophy cannot live by intuition alone. Philosophy is the *good-faith of the human spirit* with the art and the prophecy in which it currently finds nourishment. In the midst of abundant explorative riches of experience, philosophy is the resolute effort for integrity.

"And while that quest for integrity is rational, it is none the less the demand of the entire will of man, incapable of steering a clear course from an ambiguous chart.

"Among the thinkers of our century, Josiah Royce stands out for his clear sense of the task of philosophy. No one has a wider sensitivity than he for the wealth of our time in poetry, in art, in religion, in science. But he knew what philosophy must do, and what he has given us is what Professor Loewenberg has aptly called his 'Synoptic Vision,' together with the good faith and the unfailing courage with which he built an integrated dwelling for the mind and will of men, in an age more and more disposed to live in temporary shelters."

Signed: William Ernest Hocking,
July 25, 1955

This evaluation of Royce as philosopher appears to all who have known Hocking intimately to be equally applicable to Hocking himself. He possessed the same lofty qualities that he attributed to Royce.

Hocking's career ended gloriously with the completion of an unprecedented *Festschrift* volume of surpassing value. He himself collaborated with Professor Leroy S. Rouner, editor, although by curious coincidence the volume was released to the public by the publisher, Martinus Nijhoff, The Hague, Netherlands, almost on the day of Hocking's death. This volume is entitled *Philosophy, Religion, and the Coming World Civilization: Essays in Honor of William Ernest Hocking.* In a letter to the *Festschrift* contributors (July 18, 1966) the editor wrote that a special leather-bound presentation copy of the book was mailed to Professor Richard Hocking in April to give to his father, and that it was received by the senior philosopher with much pleasure. Parts of the book were read to him almost daily by members of his immediate family during his terminal illness. Rouner notes in his letter: "Hocking had seen and read the entire book in MS before publication, and had, on numerous occasions, expressed his appreciation and admiration for all of your excellent essays." The *Festschrift* volume thus contains authentic and authoritative interpretations of Hocking's philosophy and received his enthusiastic and whole-hearted approval.

The opening essay of the volume is by Rouner on "The Making of a Philosopher: Ernest Hocking's Early Years." It is a definitive biography which will always remain the primary source for anyone interested in Hocking's life and philosophy, since Rouner spent many hours with Hocking at his home in Madison, New Hampshire, conversing with him and with members of his family, and working in his private library gathering the biographical information at first hand.

Twenty-nine other essayists contributed to the *Festschrift*. Among them are distinguished philosophers including S. Rhadakrishnan, Gabriel Marcel, Marvin Farber, Raphael Demos, Charles Hartshorne, Donald Williams, Henry Nelson Wieman, H. P. Van Dusen, F. S. C. Northrop, Charles Moore, Crane Brinton, Neils Ferré, John E. Smith, Andrew J. Reck, Charles Malik, Walter Stace, and others of prominence, all of whom knew Hocking personally. Each essay shows the impact of Hocking's thinking upon the mind of its author and gives original interpretations of his teachings.

Another interesting feature of this volume is the completion of the dialogue between Hocking and Marcel in the latter's essay entitled "Solipsism Surmounted," an essay which Rouner testifies especially delighted Hocking. This dialogue began with the essay, "Gabriel Marcel and the Ground Issues of Metaphysics," published in *Philosophy and Phenomenological Research* (Vol. XIV, June, 1954, pp. 439-469), one of the most profound philosophical essays Hocking wrote. As was explained above, it was because of his deep interest in Marcel that arrangements were made for an English edition of the masterly treatise, *Royce's Metaphysics*. Hocking contributed the Preface and Marcel wrote a special Introduction to this edition (Chicago, Henry Regnery Co., 1956). In the *Festschrift* essay, "Solipsism Surmounted," we find the completion of this important dialogue.

The final evaluation of Hocking by Gabriel Marcel in this essay is worthy of careful consideration. "I hope that I have said enough to show not only the originality but the essential soundness of his thought. I should like to conclude by emphasizing this health and wholeness. I consider it extremely serious that this quality is so often lacking in contemporary thinkers, and is no longer recognized as a value. To be guilty of this denial of the best that is in us, of the most vital tradition of Western thought,

On the Centenary Year of Royce's birth

Great art requires two qualities: a true perception of the enduring meaning of common things, and an incorruptible veracity in reporting that meaning. Great philosophy requires these two and one more: beside the vision and the veracity of the artist, philosophy requires the indomitable pursuit of considering the vision, within a single conspectus of the whole.

The artist and the prophet are justified in living by intuition, reporting their perceptions one by one — not with a contempt for consistency, but in the faith that what a growing experience reveals will in time reveal itself to our coherence. But philosophy cannot live by intuition alone. Philosophy is the good-faith of the human spirit—with the art and the prophecy in which it currently finds nourishment. In the midst of whatever speculative riches of experience, philosophy is the resolute effort for integrity.

And while that good-faith integrity is rational, it is none the less the demand of the entire will of man, incapable of steering a clear course from an ambiguous chart.

Among the thinkers of our century, Josiah Royce stands out for his clear sense of the task of philosophy. No one had a wider sensitivity than the for the wealth of our time in twenty in art, in religion, in science. But he knew what philosophy must do, and what he has given us in what professors-contemporaries has fifty decays he "Synoptic Vision": Together with the good faith and the unfailing courage with which he built an interpreted dwelling for the mind) and will of man, in an age more and more disposed to live in temporary shelter

William Ernest Hocking July 25, 1955

is to carry into the realm of the spirit those processes of disintegration which, although they may have contributed to modern industrialization, now threaten to destroy our planet. Man finds himself confronted by the most decisive choice which has ever faced him in the course of his history, and it is only through the capacity for inner health and wholeness that he will be able to escape the danger of annihilation which he has brought on himself. I know of no one in our time who is better able than W. E. Hocking to set us on the way of salvation—a narrow way over the abyss."

One of the essayists is the distinguished research physicist, Frederick Werner, whose lengthy essay on "Integrity," with its valuable footnotes, indicates that Hocking's conception of the self as a "Field of Fields" can gain deeper significance by being "regarded as formally identical with some features of the objectively verified physical theory of Quantum Mechanics." He puts the crucial question: "Might Quantum Physics provide fresh insight for Hocking's as yet unfinished metaphysics?" and answers it affirmatively. That Hocking was deeply concerned and was closely cooperating with Werner is shown by his comment in a letter I received dated September 22nd, 1964. "Just now I am engaged in two rather exacting undertakings, putting the Gifford Lectures into order, and coming to terms with the newer developments of atomic physics. There is at Xavier University in Cincinnati a remarkable young physicist, Frederick Werner, who has been close to Niels Bohr, both here and in Copenhagen, and who is convinced that the paradox of 'Complementarity' needs a metaphysical answer, and some reference to the 'union of opposites.' He is making some use of my view of the Self as a 'field of fields'; and so we get together occasionally for deep plotting to introduce metaphysics into physics without creating a communist revolution in cosmology. But this is another story, except that it constitutes another motive for not wanting to leave the scene until these fascinating chores are finished."

At the editor's urging, Hocking was persuaded to include in the *Festschrift* a revision of his lecture notes for the Second Series of his Gifford Lectures. Regrettably the pressure of essential work prevented him from completing for publication his two series of Gifford Lectures. Notes of these Lectures appeared in mimeographed form in Glasgow in 1938, under the title *Fact and Destiny*. The notes on the First Series were revised by Hocking and published in the *Review of Metaphysics*, Vol. IV, pp. 1-

12, and 319-342, under the same title. (See also his Presidential address at the ninth meeting of the Metaphysical Society of America in the *Journal of Metaphysics,* Vol. XI, pp. 525-549, entitled: "Fact, Field and Destiny: The Inductive Element in Metaphysics.") Now Hocking himself has revised the notes of the Second Series, utilizing the fairly extensive condensations of the lectures he had given to the Glasgow press. Thus his own final revision of these highly significant lectures is now available in this *Festschrift* volume under the title "History and the Absolute." (pp. 423-465) Fortunately he lived to finish what he himself designated a fascinating chore.

In addition to the essays, the book contains a complete annotated bibliography of all 294 of Hocking's writings, arranged chronologically. This bibliography is definitive and of indispensable reference value. The author, Dr. Richard C. Gilman, now president of Occidental College, explains in the Foreword that when he was professor of philosophy at Colby College in 1951, he collaborated with Hocking in the preparation of the first edition of this bibliography which was printed by the College. A start on it had been made earlier while he was serving as assistant to Hocking at Dartmouth College. Now it has been brought down to date. Dr. Gilman writes that Hocking "has personally checked the present edition."

In the spring of 1936, Hocking and his charming and vivacious wife, Agnes, spent a memorable week as guests of Indiana University on the Bloomington Campus, inaugurating at my invitation the Mahlon Powell Foundation series of philosophy lectures. I edited these lectures and they were published by Yale University Press in 1937 under the title, *The Lasting Elements of Individualism.* Hocking dedicated the volume to John Dewey, "comrade and opponent through many years of deepening affection." The inscription Hocking penned in my own copy of this volume is one I cherish: "To Professor D. S. Robinson an offering of first fruits of labors as colleagues in a common task with many grateful remembrances." In 1939 the Mahlon Powell lectures appeared in a Swedish translation. They rank in importance among his minor works with his Terry Lectures at Yale University titled *The Self, Its Body, and Its Freedom* (1928), and with the McNair Lectures at the University of North Carolina, *Science and the Idea of God* (1944). *The Meaning of God in Human Experience* (Yale Press, 1912, 1963) remains his *magnum opus,* although *Human Nature and Its Remaking* (Yale

Press, 1918, Revised Edition, 1923), *Man and the State* (Yale Press, 1926), *The Spirit of World Politics* (Macmillan, 1932), *Experiment in Education* (Regnery, 1954), *The Coming World Civilization* (Harper, 1956), and *Strength of Men and Nations* (Harper, 1959) are distinctly major contributions to philosophical literature. Indeed this is true of many of the 294 items listed in the bibliography.

Hocking's booklet entitled *The Present Status of the Philosophy of Law and of Rights* (Yale Press, 1926) explains the jural postulates, developed by him in cooperation with Dean Roscoe Pound, which are the legal principles they thought essential to the very existence, as well as to the healthy functioning of any civilized society. These principles include the right of every citizen to self-realization and self-management, to the fruits of his labors and contracts, and to security. These postulates have been ignored and neglected to the detriment of our nation. Among the best textbooks introducing students to philosophy is his widely used *Types of Philosophy* (Scribners, 1929, Third Edition, 1959). Hocking's *Rethinking Missions* (Harper, 1932) and *Freedom of the Press* (University of Chicago Press, 1947) are outside the philosophical disciplines, but they illustrate his influence in promoting the common good.

While concurring in the evaluation of Marcel quoted above, I wish to add that William Ernest Hocking, in an era when many of his colleagues were hostile to dialectics and metaphysics, was himself a masterful dialectician and a consistent metaphysician. Always respectful of his critics he devoted his long life-span to a sincere quest for essential truth about ultimate reality. Personally he was hospitable and magnanimous, and a man of the highest integrity.[1]

---

[1] Reprinted from *Philosophy and Phenomenological Research*, Vol. XXVII, March, 1967, pp. 461-466.

VIII

HOCKING'S CONTRIBUTION TO
METAPHYSICAL IDEALISM

Some wise man has said: "Never regret growing old, for it is a privilege denied many." In the case of William Ernest Hocking, ninety years of age gave him the exceptional privilege of writing a Preface to the 1963 edition of *The Meaning of God in Human Experience*,[1] with the knowledge that it had become widely recognized as an unquestioned philosophic classic of the 20th Century.

In that Preface, written just fifty years after the publication of his *magnum opus*, he writes: "Modernity completely failed to resolve the dilemma of 'solipsism'; and with its inability to find an experience of other selves would follow its deeper inability to find an experience of God. I had for some time been of the belief that these barriers could be surmounted and that they would fall together. In my own experience they did; this book is to that extent autobiographical."[2]

Undoubtedly, one of the most enlightening autobiographical statements in the *Meaning of God in Human Experience* vividly describes his own experience of other selves or minds: "I have sometimes sat looking at a comrade speculating on this mysterious isolation of self from self. Why are we so made that I gaze and see of thee only thy Wall, and never Thee? This Wall of thee is but a movable part of the Wall of my world; and I also am a Wall to thee: we look out at one another from behind masks. How would it seem if my mind could but once be *within* thine; and we could meet and without barrier be with each other? And then it has fallen upon me like a shock—as when one thinking himself alone has felt a presence—But I *am* in thy soul. These things round me are in thy experience. They are thy own; when I touch them and move them I change *thee*. When I look on them

---

[1] 14th ed.

[2] *Ibid.*, p. xii.

I see what thou seest; when I listen I hear what thou hearest. I am in the great Room of thy soul; and I experience thy very experience. For *where art thou?* Not there, behind those eyes, within that head, in darkness, fraternizing with chemical processes. Of these, in my own case, I know nothing, and will know nothing; for my existence is spent not behind my Wall but in front of it. I am there where I have treasures. And there art thou also. This world in which I live, is the world of thy soul: and being within that, I am within thee. I can imagine no contact more real and thrilling than this; that we should meet and share identity, not through ineffable inner depths (alone), but here through the foregrounds of common experience; and that thou shouldst be—not behind that mask—but *here,* pressing with all thy consciousness upon me, *containing* me, and these things of mine. This is reality: and having seen it thus, I can never again be frightened into monadism by reflections which have strayed from their guiding insight.'"[3]

This entire passage from Hocking's book is quoted by R. F. A. Hoernlé in *Contemporary Metaphysics*[4] with the comment that it has the "effect of fresh observation." Since our objective is to state clearly the major contribution of Hocking to idealistic metaphysics, suppose we follow up this clue suggested by Hoernlé by imagining some seekers of the year A.D. 2264 reading this quotation in *Contemporary Metaphysics,* and earnestly desiring more information about its author's philosophy, finding this volume of essays commemorating Hocking's life work. What can we tell him that will give him a somewhat clearer idea of the thought that underlies this autobiographical statement?

First, let us summarize for our hypothetical seeker of A.D. 2264, the idealistic metaphysics implicit in this autobiographical statement, and permeating the whole book. All three of the basic objects of human knowledge: God, Nature, and our fellowmen are on an equal footing. They are not to be regarded as independent objects of cognition. Each is more or less involved in and with the other. However, consciousness of the reality of any one of these objects is supported by our consciousness of the reality of the other two. Nature and natural objects in general are only known to us to be real because they are the common objects

---

[3] *Ibid.*, pp. 265 f. Hocking told Professor Leroy Rouner that his "comrade" in this experience was Agnes Hocking.

[4] pp. 229 f.

known by other selves. Likewise selves are only known to us as real because they are fellow knowers of these natural objects. Nature and natural objects, as well as the conceptual objects of logic and mathematics, and also other selves are all known to be real only because there is implicitly present in our knowledge of each such object that great other self whom we call God. From the beginning, Hocking says, "God then is immediately known, and permanently known, as the Other mind which in creating Nature is also creating me."[5]

This idealistic metaphysics can be clarified for our seeker of A.D. 2264 by another highly significant autobiographical account of Hocking's classroom relation to his revered teacher, Josiah Royce. In his Preface for the English translation of Gabriel Marcel's *Royce's Metaphysics,* Hocking wrote: "In an essay submitted to him (Royce) during my last graduate year at Harvard, 1903-04, I ventured to differ from one of his central doctrines, namely, that we have no direct knowledge either of our own minds or of other minds. For, as he held, selves are individual; and individuals are beings such that, for each one, there can be in the whole universe no other precisely like it; this is what we mean by our individual attachments. Such uniqueness can be no matter of empirical knowledge: it is rather a matter of will: it is thus that the mother says, 'There shall be no child like my child' *(The World and the Individual,* 458-460) *ergo* no possible substitution, no recompense for loss. In this particular essay, I reported an experience in which, as I read it, I was directly aware of another mind and my own as co-knowers of an 'It.' So far as feeling was involved, that *feeling was cognitive,* not simply an I-will: we must extend the conception of empirical knowledge, and so admit an element of realism within the ideal totality. I was expecting a radical criticism from my revered professor. Instead, when Royce handed my essay back, he pointed out the dissenting passage with the comment, 'This is your insight: you must adhere to that!' Without assenting to my view, he had given me his blessing for its development."[6]

Let our seeker of A.D. 2264 note especially that Hocking here makes four incisive criticisms of Royce's metaphysical idealism. First, he implies that Royce was mistaken in thinking that the

---

[5] *The Meaning of God in Human Experience,* p. 297.

[6] Gabriel Marcel, *Royce's Metaphysics* (Chicago, Henry Regnery Co., 1956), p. vii f.

major theses of metaphysical idealism are capable of dialectical proof. Second, he mistakenly held that we have no direct knowledge either of our own minds or of other minds. Thirdly, in support of this second thesis, Royce held that each mind is too uniquely individual to be known directly. Fourthly, he claimed that, will being the essence of this uniqueness, empirical knowledge of it is impossible. This explains Royce's insistence that self knowledge is neither perceptual nor conceptual, but interpretative. His highly original theory of interpretation is used by him to explain both self-knowledge and knowledge of other selves. Now consider the way in which Hocking attacked this central tendency in Royce's idealistic metaphysics. He reported an experience of his own which contradicted it, and used it to prove that feeling is cognitive, not simply an I-will but an I-know you—another mind. Instead of replying to this with a radical rebuttal, Royce called Hocking's experience and argument an insight to which Hocking must adhere.

Surely this second autobiographical statement explains the first. Hence the original statement of his position was in an essay submitted to Royce's graduate class in Metaphysics where it received Royce's blessing.

Our hypothetical seeker of the year A.D. 2264 will also be interested in the following bit of information about Hocking's unpublished doctoral dissertation submitted to the Harvard University Faculty of Philosophy in 1904. This is only available in the Widener Library. It is entitled "The Elementary Experience of Other Conscious Being in Its relation to the Elementary Experience of Physical and Reflexive Objects." This was written in the author's thirty-first year or sixty years ago. Richard C. Gilman's *The Bibliography of William Ernest Hocking from 1898-1951* contains this important descriptive comment: "A note above the title describes it as 'Philosophy of Communication, Part I,' thus announcing its central theme and indicating the author's further plans for research and publication on that topic. The main thesis of this work, which might be restated as 'How We Know Other Minds,' is the original statement of Chapters XVII to XX of *The Meaning of God in Human Experience*." The chapter headings to which Gilman refers are XVII, "The Knowledge of Other Minds than Our Own"; XVIII, "Such Knowledge as We Could Desire"; XIX, "That Knowledge We Have"; and XX, "Our Natural Realism and Realism Absolute."

Surely this will make it quite clear to our hypothetical seeker of A.D. 2264 that Hocking elaborated the essay written for Royce's graduate class in Metaphysics for the academic year 1903-04 into his doctor's dissertation submitted at the end of that academic term, and later incorporated the central portions of that dissertation in the first edition of *The Meaning of God in Human Experience* (1912).

For the benefit of other seekers as well as our A.D. 2264 seeker after knowledge about Hocking, I will now support this conclusion with another most significant autobiographical account of his study in Germany before completing his doctoral dissertation. He spent three months studying with Edmund Husserl at Göttingen in late 1902 and early 1903, on a Harvard Fellowship for travel and study abroad. In telling about this in the Volume commemorating the centennial year of Husserl's birth,[7] he pays tribute to Husserl for initiating what he calls "the widened empiricism of a new 'opening era of thought'." Referring to his article, "Marcel and the Ground Issues of Metaphysics,"[8] he writes: "I have recently compared Husserl and Marcel in regard to the structure of experience." He explains that he has now come to see that "we must add for the further-widened empiricism of our opening era, a just recognition of the presence in experience of *three aspects of metaphysical reality*—the Self, the Other, and the Thou.

"It was these metaphysical aspects of experience of which I was in search, and for which I found in the Husserl of that day no satisfactory light. I had already prior to my year in Germany been concerned with the theoretical problem of solipsism, for which neither Royce nor James had a solution. I had flung out a vague sketch of a future doctoral thesis on the 'Philosophy of Communication, Part I: The Knowledge of Other Minds.' I continued to search Husserl's thought and writings for a theory of the role of the Ego in phenomenological enquiry, and of the Alter-ego seemingly presupposed in our assumption that the world of nature perceived by each is identical for all, —the universality of the private object.

"For Royce, Self and Other-self are not empirically given. They are objects of purpose, or moral resolve. I do not perceive, nor can I prove, my own identity from day to day: but as a matter of common decency I *hold myself responsible* as the same in-

---

[7] *Edmund Husserl, 1859-1959* (La Haye, Martinus Nijhoff), 1959.

[8] *Philosophy and Phenomenological Research*, Vol. 14, pp. 439 ff.

dividual as he who gave you the promise yesterday. At the same time, I *will* to regard *you*—though I cannot experience nor prove it—as the same individual as he to whom yesterday I gave the promise. For Münsterberg, as for Fichte, the Other-self is an entity *acknowledged,* not given in any perception whatever. For Husserl, I seemed to find these matters still unresolved, in *Werden.* . . . There were rooted convictions that continued to hold their own in my mind: as that the Self is both concept and experience; that it is both elemental and unique; that its complexity, which is genuine, is compatible with its simplicity of essence, and must be approached by way of its immediate simplicity. . . . The following year at Harvard (1903-04), devoted to my doctoral thesis, explored the problem of the Self and the Other-Self, a frontal attack on the problem of solipsism. The substance of that thesis, proposing a valid Intersubjectivity whose recognition, I believe, characterizes the present philosophical era, was published in 1912, as *The Meaning of God in Human Experience.''*

It should be added that the copy of his book which he inscribed and sent to Husserl is now in the *Husserl-Archief* at Louvain, along with photostatic copies of most of the letters they exchanged.

Let me remind our hypothetical A.D. 2264 seeker that the above account is supported by some highly significant comments of Gabriel Marcel in the Foreword to the English Edition of his now classic treatise, *Royce's Metaphysics,* to which Hocking wrote the Preface from which we quoted above. ''Several years before I began to study Royce I had read not only Bradley's *Appearance and Reality and Essays on Truth and Reality,* but also the *magnum opus* of W. E. Hocking, *The Meaning of God in Human Experience,* which, I am sure, had a lasting influence on me. But it cannot be doubted that Hocking's book was an advance of Royce's thought, an advance in the direction of that metaphysical realism toward which I resolutely tended. Had these encounters succeeded one another in logical order, I should have read Royce before reading Hocking. But such was not the case.''

In his Conclusion, Marcel states three alternatives with respect to the relation of God to history and to individual conscious experience. One alternative is to claim that God or the Absolute is aloof from all human experience; the antithesis of this is the theory that God or the Absolute is implicated in every human experience; and the third alternative is an attempted reconciliation or synthesis of these two contradictory aspects in an over-rigid unity or system which Marcel thinks fails to do justice to each individual consciousness.

Then the author states his own theistic existentialist solution of this problem, relating it to the position of Royce and Hocking. He writes: "The theory of participation in Being, some of whose important elements we have found in Royce, and which has been made precise by W. E. Hocking, allows us to transcend the three alternatives we have just expounded in that it is oriented towards a definite rejection of those categories that are inadequate to the proper object of metaphysics, and towards a less systematic, but more faithful and profound, interpretation of our spiritual life. A philosophy of this kind, which ceases to demand from reality guarantees that inevitably turn into fetters, tends expressly to acknowledge an order of freedom and love in which the relation of being to being, far from integrating in a single rational system, which after all, will never be more than a convention, would remain the expression of separate but social persons who partake of God to the extent that they believe in Him."[9] Here again, Marcel indicates how Hocking made Royce's position more precise.

Now let me explain to our A.D. 2264 seeker that, when *The Meaning of God in Human Experience* was published in 1912, one of its most acute critics was the late Dr. Douglas Clyde Macintosh, **Professor of Systematic Theology at the Yale Divinity** School. At that time Hocking was a member of the staff of the Department of Philosophy at Yale University. Macintosh contributed an article entitled "Hocking's Philosophy of Religion: An Empirical Development of Absolutism" to the *Philosophical Review,* [10] excerpts from which he later included in his extended critical exposition of what he calls Hocking's "Mystical-logical-psychological Idealism" in his scholarly volume: *The Problem of Knowledge.*[11] He considers Hocking's book to be "an empirical development of absolutism," claims that Hocking's Absolute actually is a synthesis of the three elemental types of idealism: the psychological (Berkeley), the logical (Hegel, Royce, Bradley and Bosanquet), and the mystical (A. E. Taylor). Macintosh rightly claims that Hocking argues that feeling, and especially religious

---

[9] Marcel, *op. cit.*, p. 155.

[10] Vol. XXIII, 1914, pp. 27-42.

[11] New York, The Macmillan Co., 1915, Chp. VIII.

worship and mystical ecstasy as described by the great saints and mystics, is cognitive and that he supports this theory with an ingenious dialectical argument and an analysis of the experience of the great mystics. Macintosh's careful presentation of his case against Hocking is worthy of thoughtful consideration and more attention than it has hitherto received. Hocking informed me that he never answered him. Macintosh writes from the point of view of critical realism. He admits that "Hocking's philosophy may be regarded as, in principle, the consummation of the idealistic way of thinking." Both in this volume and in his later *Theology as an Empirical Science*[12] he accepts Hocking's transformation of the ontological argument for the existence of God from a deductive to an empirical type of argument. Even though it was originated by St. Anselm, as amended by Hocking, Macintosh considers it to be still "tainted with Hegelianism."

Our seeker of A.D. 2264 will be especially interested to learn that one of the chief criticisms directed against Hocking by Macintosh deals with a part of the first autobiographical statement quoted above which he designates "an inference from a report of analysis of social experience." First Macintosh quotes five sentences from Hocking's statement. "I *am* in thy soul. These things around me are in thy experience. They are thy own; when I touch them and move them I change *thee*. When I look on them I see what thou seest; when I listen I hear what thou hearest. I am in the great room of thy soul; and I experience thy very experience." Then he comments as follows: "Here it would seem that, owing to the failure to develop a critical realism (such as we shall defend in a later chapter) instead of the natural realism rendered untenable by psychology, it is assumed that as two persons have immediate perceptual knowledge of a certain object, and as the object is not two, but one, they must each be in the soul of the other, or both in the same soul, as in a 'room.' If now we get rid of this spatial conception of consciousness, and view all conscious process as a creative activity of the self, through which even the sense-qualities of the object are produced, though not the physical energy undergoing transformation in space and time it becomes clear that two minds can, similarly and simultaneously, immediately experience the same thing, without these minds interpenetrating each other. Each simply clothes one and the same physical object with similar sense-qualities, only each

---

[12] New York, The Macmillan Co., 1919, p. 93.

does it for himself alone. On Hocking's view as above expressed, if we were to take it at all literally, and in conjunction with his doctrine of the non-dependence of secondary qualities of physical objects upon the sensing subject, it would be difficult to explain how it is that when I view a colored object which is being perceived at the same time by a color-blind person, I see it not at all differently from the way in which it presents itself when I view it with another person of normal visual powers. In the former case at least it is not true that 'I experience thy very experience.' "[13]

Certainly Hocking would agree that his spatial conception of consciousness is entirely inadequate and is not to be taken literally. Certainly he would also agree with his critic that "all conscious process is a creative activity of the self," although he would undoubtedly deny that "each does it for himself alone." Nor would Hocking have any trouble disposing of Macintosh's argument about the color-blind or other abnormal persons since any intelligent color-blind person can understand and communicate to others what normal color vision is. Nevertheless, these criticisms of Macintosh show how Hocking's doctrines were received when his book was first published.

Another critic of Hocking's theory that knowledge of other minds presupposes and requires a knowledge of the Absolute Mind is my fellow-contributor to this volume, Y. H. Krikorian, who writes from the standpoint of naturalistic humanism.[14] For the benefit of our hypothetical seeker of A.D. 2264, as well as other seekers, his essay is especially worthy of examination, since it is answered by Hocking in his "Response to Professor Krikorian's Discussion."[15]

There are two dilemmas of modernity that are the basic trouble of contemporary civilization because they block the efforts of religion to provide adequate motivation for human living. The first arises from subjectivity which shrinks each person within himself and the second arises from objectivity which results in a mechanized and purposeless universe because it rests solely upon the abstract universals of science. Hocking attempts to escape

---

[13] *Ibid.*, p. 168.

[14] *Journal of Philosophy*, Vol. LV, March, 1958, pp. 275-280 (For Krikorian's essay, see Leroy Rouner's Festschrift Volume: *Philosophy, Religion, and the Coming World Civilization*, pp. 49-58.

[15] *Ibid.*

from both of these dilemmas of modernity by his emphasis upon
direct knowledge of the Absolute as we find this in religious worship, and especially in the quest for ecstasy of the great mystics.
Krikorian recognizes that there is considerable merit in this
analysis, when he writes: "One must agree with Hocking that
the integrity of civilization needs some source of motivation."
Although his article is based primarily on Hocking's *The Coming
World Civilization* he quotes approvingly a part of the very
same passage from *The Meaning of God in Human Experience*
that was quoted above by me, and also, in part by Macintosh to
whom he refers in a footnote. But he finally concludes: "Yet if
the critical analysis that has been offered is acceptable, subjectivity may be transcended without resort to a cosmic Mind as
the creator of Nature and the sustainer of universal judgments;
the objectivity of science may be admitted without fear of *its*
abstractions; and the idea of the whole may be used as regulative
ideal without supernatural implications. If these claims are true,
then the source of motivation for humanity must be found within
the natural setting for its existence—in experimental intelligence, in enlightened morality, and in art rather than in something beyond them which is neither verifiable or approachable."

Admitting that Krikorian's comments are clear, central and
just, Hocking answers him by developing what he calls the "concept with a *double boundary.*" He writes: "Through the clarity
of Professor Krikorian's critique, the issues between us appear
in definite relief. I venture to locate the main issue in terms of
a question, 'Why is not Nature enough, without Supernature?'
Krikorian's answer is, I take it, 'Nature is enough; Supernature
is superfluous.' My answer would be, 'There *is* a Nature that is
enough; but *that* Nature includes Supernature, together with
modernity's (and perhaps Krikorian's) Nature; it is a concept
with *a double boundary.*' "[16] Hocking claims that the crucial
question is whether there is a con-natural character of nature
best explained by a single but quite essential question: "Is our
conscious awareness of Nature a part of Nature?" If the answer
is "Yes," Nature means one thing, and if the answer is "No,"
Nature means another thing. Hence Krikorian's concept of Nature is a concept with a double boundary.

Hocking writes: "How, then, do I answer the question
whether perceiving is a part of Nature?

---

[16] *Ibid.*, p. 275 f.

"I answer Yes: there certainly is a Nature which includes the brain-processes which symbolize perception, processes which co-vary with variables of perceiving. *And No:* the knowing of that Nature is not part of the Nature then-and-there known. This knowing-awareness is strictly extra-natural, in a sense corres-ponding to that in which the Nature-observed is extra-mental. But the mutual otherness here insisted on, as between observing process and Nature observed, is a *natural relation,* a comment which brings us back to our affirmation, on another plane.

"For it implies that there is a wider Nature—one which in-cludes with the Nature-of-physical-science the observing process (together with all other aspects of concrete awareness such as end-seeking, feeling, deciding). This wider Nature unites Na-ture-sub-one with its negation, the non-natural, or extra-natural, or, if one prefers, super-natural.

"In brief, 'Nature' is one of a group of concepts, crucial in metaphysical enquiry, to which I have referred as 'concepts with a double boundary.' Such a concept in its wider sense includes its own narrower sense together with the opposite of the narrow-er: N_2 includes N_1 with not-N_1: the 'synthesis' *is the thesis* re-defined.''[17]

Thus the concept with a double boundary turns out to be the dialectical method. It is effectively used in all of Hocking's writings, and it is difficult, indeed, for any critic to escape its rapier-like thrusts.[18]

---

[17] *Ibid.,* pp. 278 f.

[18] In conclusion, let me call attention to my own writings in which I have discussed special doctrines and ideas of Hocking. In the essay "Philosophy of Religion in the United States since 1900," contributed to *Philosophic Thought in France and the United States,* edited by Marvin Farber, (Buffalo, The University of Buffalo Press, 1950), I have expounded his philosophy of religion. Consult also the index of my *God of the Liberal Christian,* (New York, Appleton, 1926). My essay entitled "Hocking's Political Philosophy" first appeared in *The Personalist,* Vol. XXVIII, pp. 147-160, and was reprinted in Chapter V of *Crucial Issues in Philosophy* (Christopher Pub-lishing House, Boston, 1955). I expounded his jural and ethical postulates and other basic political and ethical principles in my *Political Ethics* (T. Y. Crowell, N.Y., 1935). His theory of three orders, based on deep human urges or needs—the Private Order, based on sex-love and filial love, the Public Order, based on ambition, and the Cultural Order, based on human creativity, is expounded at length in my *Principles of Conduct* (Appleton-Century-Crofts, New York, 1948).

Nearly all of his Presidential address to the American Philosophical association is included in my *Anthology of Recent Philosophy* (Thomas

The above account of "Hocking's Contribution to Idealistic Metaphysics" was mailed to Professor Hocking with a letter requesting him to confirm the autobiographical details it contains. In his reply, written at his home in Madison, New Hampshire, and dated 22nd September 1964, he writes:

"There is nothing I would want to alter in these pages .... I am particularly grateful to you for your recovery of the Macintosh criticism: all that you say about that is helpful and just. The spatial language of my report in *The Meaning of God* is both inadequate and misleading. Yet it is hard to find an equivalent for the metaphorical 'within.' Whitehead finds the same difficulty in that important passage in which he reverses his denial that the world can be 'in the mind' in *Nature and Life:* 'Thus, in a sense, the experienced world is one complex factor in the composition of many factors constituting the essence of the soul. We can phrase this shortly by saying that in one sense the world is in the soul, (p. 40). He refers later on the same page to 'this baffling antithetical relation' whereby I am in the room and in another sense the room is in me!"

Inasmuch as I discussed above Hocking's tribute to his revered teacher, Josiah Royce, it is especially fitting that this essay should close with his comment on a significant statement of his esteemed colleague, Alfred North Whitehead.

I am grateful to Professor Hocking for his confirmation and his informative comments, and for his gracious permission to append them here.

Crowell, 1929) under the title, "What Philosophy Says." My review of his *Experiment in Education* (Chicago, Regnery, 1954) appeared in *Philosophy and Phenomenological Research*, Vol. XV, pp. 424-426.

These various discussions of Hocking show the profound influence he has exercised on my thinking since I first attended his graduate class in philosophy at Yale University over a half century ago.

IX

HOCKING'S POLITICAL PHILOSOPHY

William Ernest Hocking's philosophy is deeply rooted in his mystical idealistic metaphysics, which he learned at Harvard University especially from the two skillful teachers and original thinkers, Professors Josiah Royce and George Herbert Palmer, but which he freshly formulated in a strikingly original manner in his first treatise which was entitled: *The Meaning of God in Human Experience.* Now this metaphysics is itself a significant part of what has come to be known as Anglo-American Idealism which is deeply rooted in the epoch-making movement known as Post-Kantian idealism, especially as this was represented by the rationalists, Fichte, Schelling and Hegel, and by the irrationalist and pessimist, Arthur Schopenhauer. But this major epistemological form of absolutism is in turn deeply rooted in the idealism which was originally firmly established by Plato and Aristotle, and was continued on into modern times by a succession of first-rate philosophers from Plotinus through St. Augustine, St. Thomas Aquinas, and Bruno to Spinoza. This whole movement, from the Greek philosophers down to our day, has been designated by Professor Urban as the Great Tradition. Now if we would understand Professor Hocking's political philosophy we must recognize that it is part and parcel of this Great Tradition. He is a contemporary representative and able defender of a voluntaristic and rationalistic conception of the State, which assumes political society to be a temporal aspect or phase of the Absolute Mind unfolding in human history.

This interesting theory is expounded and set forth in great detail in five important books, which are of the utmost significance as contributions to contemporary philosophical literature dealing with political, ethical, and legal problems. They are: (1) *Human Nature and Its Remaking,* 1st. ed. 1918, second revised edition, 1923; (2) *Man and the State,* 1926; (3) *The Present Status of the Philosophy of Law and of Rights,* 1926; (4) *The Spirit of World Politics,* with special studies of the Near East, 1932, and (5) *Lasting Elements of Individualism,* 1937. But in addition to these major treatises, Professor Hocking has contributed numerous special articles to various magazines and symposia, among which the following should be mentioned as having considerable importance in the development of his political philosophy as a whole: (1) "Ways of Thinking about Rights; a new Theory of the Relation between Law and Morals," (2) "The Future of Liberalism." (3) "America's World Purpose," (4) Articles on Political Zionism, and (5) "Part I General Principles" of *Rethinking Missions,* a Layman's Inquiry after one hundred years, by the Commission of Appraisal of which Professor Hocking was Chairman, 1932. Frequent references to and quotations from these various writings will be made as we proceed with a fuller exposition of his political philosophy.

Perhaps the best clue to Professor Hocking's conception of the State is to be found in his sociological and epistemological theory of how human beings know each other's minds. The Concept of a social matrix, composed of interpenetrating self-conscious minds or selves, is the chief cornerstone of the edifice of Professor Hocking's political philosophy. Unless we grasp the full import of this conception at the outset we are likely to find his philosophy of law and of the State somewhat baffling. The meeting of minds in any community presupposes the reality of a non-physical, spiritual over-soul as the essence of communal life. Following Plato he calls the will of each individual a micro-state. And then he explains the relationship of man to the State in three sentences:

"The will of this micro-state we call an individual is and remains *a will about what others should do,* and not alone a will about what he himself shall do. His will naturally overflows its organic banks; and what the State has to do is to canalize and unify the overflow of a million wills. *The State is this unified will surplus.*" (*Man and The State,* p. 156.)

To reach this conception of the State, Professor Hocking analyzes communal life into two basic processes, both of which are always functioning in any civilized society. These two processes are: term-making, or the arbitrational or judicial process, the functionaries of which are called politicians, and the history-making or group-making process, the functionaries of which are designated statesmen. Although it must be recognized that most functionaries in local communities combine both functions, *judgment* is the chief psychological characteristic of the politician, and *will* or the ability to get things done dominates the personality of a good statesman. Term-making arises out of the inherent and inescapable conflicts among men over economic goods and other competitive values. In working out an adjustment among members of the community that will resolve these conflicts the arbiter sets up rules which by repeated application establish customs that operate as free laws. Later these develop into statute and judge-made laws. Thus a complete legal system ultimately evolves out of the term-making process as this continually operates in any living political society. But history-making is the more important of the two processes, because it is what produces the various historic events which constitute the life of a people as they pass from a social conditon in which the intentions of the separate wills of the members are relatively dispersed to a condition where there is a relatively unified purpose. For example, when the members of a community act together to achieve specific results in pyramid or road building, or in any other communal project that requires cooperation this process is present. Hocking gives it the special name *commotive process* because it is a union of efforts in which all participants move together to accomplish the end proposed. This commotive process builds the administrative institutions which constitute a vital part of any political community.

Using the classic dialectical method developed by Fichte and Hegel, Professor Hocking treats these two processes as the thesis and the antithesis among social functions and then sets up the State as their synthesis. In a civilized society this synthesis is possible because there is a common political element in term-making and the commotive process, namely a rational and reflective interpretation of all group life. To express this differently, a social order advances from a purely customary level of social behavior to a reflective level where the members are self-conscious persons who have formulated a definite plan or purpose for their group; and then the social order becomes a State.

What this means is that the State is a creation of conscious human art at work in the field of politics. The interworking of term-making and the commotive process molds any community into an artificial environment. "Society," Professor Hocking writes, "becomes saturated with a self-continuing mass of judgment and practical habit, so that it has something of the regularity of the non-human environment when stabilized by clothing, shelter, heat-control, and other artifices." (*Loc. cit.*, p. 32.) This

clearly indicates that he conceives of the State as a kind of artificial social environment superimposed upon the natural physical
and biological environment—the land, sea, and air, with their
myriad forms of vegetable and animal life, and their numerous
mineral deposits. Man builds the State as an instrument with
which to control all the forces of nature, but even more to control the purely human energies which threaten to destroy man.
Professor Hocking writes:

"When we consider that there is more peril to the life and interests of any man from the pugnacity, the greed, the stupidity,
or the simple indifference of his human context than from all
other forces of nature, we have a rough measure of the advantage
of achieving stability in this domain. Such stable or partly stable
arrangements we call states." (*Loc. cit.*, p. 32.)

This was written between the two World Wars. How much
more applicability it has now, in view of the invention and use of
atomic bombs! Unless mankind can find a way to use political
processes to work out a satisfactory control over atomic bombs,
and other implements of destruction, the states that now exist
and possess vast super-powers may turn out to be the very agencies that will destroy all civilization upon this planet. Professor
Hocking is well aware of this danger, and as we shall emphasize
later he advocates an effective union of states to bring about such
control and to promote the highest possible cultural achievements. Here it is important to stress the fact that the State is
an artificial creation of human beings, the product of their co-
operative efforts to win a greater security, freedom, and justice
for all through a unification of their wills.

Professor Hocking strives earnestly to make clear the real
purpose of the State, because he considers this to be "the main
problem of political philosophy." He argues persuasively that
since a State has many functions to perform, these must certainly
be fragments of one enduring purpose. Now this purpose is a
moral end, and the several functions of the State are various
ways and means for the attainment of this end. It follows that
one can never adequately explain the State by viewing it as "a
collection of public services." He admits that most, if not all,
actual states are only able to approximate more or less a full
realization of the purpose of the State. But he insists that the
true State has an all-inclusive end or purpose and he undertakes
to explain what it is. Let us consider two different approaches

to a statement of what this goal of any State is, one an inductive approach, and the other a postulational approach.

In making the inductive approach Professor Hocking recognizes that induction has to be combined with interpretation to reach a satisfactory formulation of the purpose of the State. It is then, an interpretative induction that he seeks. But he also calls it *intuitive induction*, because it reaches its hypothesis suddenly and clearly after the mind of the investigator has been well informed about a multitude of facts. Such an intuitive induction is like the flash of insight which accompanies the vision of a religious mystic. It is the kind of intuitive understanding which the French philosopher, Bergson, recommends as the one and only source of genuine knowledge of creative evolution.

Professor Hocking examines the economic interpretation of the State, the totalitarian theory that "the State is for itself," and the idea that the State exists for the sake of culture or human civilization as a whole. But for one reason or another he rejects them all, and adopts as his own hypothesis what can rightly be named the personalistic interpretative and intuitive induction. Stated in his own words it is:

"The form of the State's aim is the making of history; its substance is the making of men. That is, it cannot make men without the long circuit of history. . . . We assert that the heart and focus of all ultimate value is in persons, not in such abstractions as society, culture, history; and that the State's purpose must find its terminus there." (*Loc. cit.*, p.174.)

"The State," he says further on, "is a territorial body of people united under a sovereign power for the purpose of making a better breed of men, by way of participating in world history and rendering more rational the inner play of social powers." (*Loc. cit.*, p. 195.)

Thus, when we carefully consider what all of the functions of the State are and mean, we can make the interpretative induction that the central aim and enduring purpose that runs through them like a red thread is the moulding of human souls, the making of men, the development of human personalities. But it must be admitted that the metaphysical doctrine behind this political philosophy is a voluntaristic and personalistic absolutism rather than a monadistic or individualistic conception of the type known as spiritual pluralism.

The postulation approach yields essentially the same conclusion, but it is more circuitous and it is developed by Professor

Hocking in a variety of ways. One of the most interesting of these is worked out in his little book entitled *The Present Status of the Philosophy of Law and Rights,* in which he shows the influence of Dean Roscoe Pound with whom he conducted at Harvard University a joint graduate seminar on the Philosophy of Law. Dean Pound formulated a set of postulates for any civilized society. They were called *jural postulates* and they are the basic ethical assumptions which underlie and undergird the statute and common law embodied in any civilized community. There are five of these jural postulates. Before stating them Professor Hocking lays down the basic ethical norm or principle of the Philosophy of Law. The norm is "the natural right of the individual to become what he is capable of becoming." Two sets of essential rights are derived from this norm; three *rights to liberty:* (1) liberty of self-management, (3) beneficent control over others, (3) control over the forces of nature, and three *rights to security:* (1) security of person, (2) security of agreements and contracts, and (3) possession of private property.

The five jural postulates embody these six essential rights of every responsible citizen. They are:

Jural postulate I

In civilized society men must be able to assume that others will commit no intentional aggressions upon them.

Jural postulate II

In civilized society men must be able to assume that they may control for beneficial purposes what they have discovered and appropriated to their own use, what they have created by their own labor, and what they have acquired under the existing social and economic order.

Jural postulate III

In civilized society men must be able to assume that those with whom they deal in the general intercourse of society will act in good faith, and hence, (a) will make good reasonable expectations which their promises or other conduct reasonably create; (b) will carry out their undertakings according to the expectations which the moral sentiment of the community attaches thereto; (c) will restore specifically or by equivalent what comes to them by mistake or unanticipated situation, whereby they may receive what they could not reasonably have expected to receive under the actual circumstances.

Jural postulate IV

In civilized society men must be able to assume that others, when they act affirmatively, will do so with due care with respect to consequences that may be reasonably anticipated.

Jural postulate V

In civilized society men must be able to assume that others who maintain things likely to get out of hand or to escape and do damage will restrain them within their proper bounds. *The Present Status of the Philosophy of Law and of Rights,* pp. 93f.

Elsewhere Professor Hocking made another attempt to establish these jural postulates as implication of one basic norm or principle, and he calls this "a new theory of the relation between law and morals." He thinks that political philosophy has a special interest in and concern with that general field of social thought where law and ethics meet and intermingle. Yet one cannot simply identify law and morals "for law requires while morals leave free, and law casts into a general social mold what morals propose as individual duty." He proposes the essential principle of the *value of valuers* as the ultimate postulate on which law and ethics rest. "There is," he writes, "one thing in any society that is worth more than the goods which that society possesses, namely, the capacity of appreciating those goods, a capacity that resides only in individual persons." [1]

It follows that there is an ultimate postulate as to the *value of valuers* which can be stated in this way: "The normal conditions of personal growth are necessary conditions for any social welfare." This is really the ethical basis of every civilized society, and it coincides with the norm previously stated that the State exists primarily as an embodiment of the purpose or aim to enable every individual citizen to become all that he is capable of becoming. It would be suicidal for any civilized community to reject this postulate as defining its purpose because "its whole being and its future must be derived from the growing points of personality." Thus in this undergirding postulate Professor Hocking restates the purpose of the State

---

[1] See *Law: A Century of Progress*, 1835-1935. Vol. II, p. 263.

which he reached by using the intuitive and interpretative inductive approach.

Consequently, no matter which of the two alternative approaches to the formulation of the State's purpose is used, we are led in either case to the view that the State exists in order that it may provide the institutionalized means and agencies that will enable its members to attain the fullest possible development of their personalities. The furthering of personal life is the final goal and purpose of each and every civilized society. No other end can ever supplant this basic moral aim.

It is an interesting fact that Professor Hocking has recently extended this conception of the purpose of the State to include the establishment of a genuine international order in which men can "make visible the resolve of the nations to live under law and to set up the first law: 'the law that there shall be law'." In an important article entitled "America's World Purpose" which was written during World War II and was quite widely distributed among service personnel by the Servicemen's Christian League, he calls upon American citizens to turn "their native characteristics and qualities of temperament into a positive policy and keep our present appointment with destiny." And what are these native characteristics and qualities of temperament? They consist of a "peculiar ability to take the other man's point of view," "faith in man," and "native shrewdness, factuality and inventiveness." And what is our nation's present appointment with destiny? To contribute to the peoples of the earth what we have discovered to be the end and goal of any civilized community, and to win them to an adoption of this purpose as the common good of all mankind. And this means that we must give full support to the creation of the kind of an International World Order which will value valuers above economic goods and which will further everywhere and to the fullest possible extent the development of moral and spiritual personalities.

Between the two World Wars Professor Hocking was sent to the Near East by the Bureau of International Research of Harvard University and Radcliffe College to make a first-hand study of the working of the mandates of the League of Nations in that area. His important book, *The Spirit of World Politics,* grew out of that experience and research. In Part V of this book he subjected Political Zionism to searching examination and advocated Cultural Zionism as a substitute. He expressed sympathy with the Arabs in the tense situation created by the establishment of a Jewish State in Palestine, and the purchase by Jews of the bulk of the best agricultural areas around Jerusalem. Taking this stand on the Jewish question brought him into controversy with his colleague on the Faculty of Harvard University, Mr. Felix Frankfurter. In this controversy Professor Hocking ably defended his position, and so far as I know he has never been in favor of Political Zionism. He proposed that the Holy Land be administered by the League of Nations as a kind of international shrine for the three great religions to which Jerusalem is sacred, Judaism, Christianity, and Mohammedanism.

Certainly Hocking's careful studies in *The Spirit of World Politics* of the Near East, in the early period of the development of the Israeli nation, are of permanent value to students seeking background knowledge for an understanding of the crucial unsettled social and political issues facing the Jewish people and the Arab nations, following the June War of 1967, and the cease-fire armistice agreement now in effect in that area.

However, the Zionist discussions are insignificant alongside of the original development of political ethics which *The Spirit of World Politics* contains. Professor Hocking subjected French rule in Syria and British rule in Egypt to severe criticism. He exposed the weaknesses in the doctrine of economic imperialism —which means a progressive people claiming the right to exploit the resources of areas occupied by backward peoples for the benefit of the exploiting nation. This is preceded by an analysis and evaluation of the distinction between backward and progressive peoples in which he formulated standards of measurement of backwardness. These include such things as "the mastery of nature," the condition of "public morality" and "the condition of the common people." He worked out a basic principle and aplied it to the relations of progressive nations to backward peoples. The negative form of that ethical principle is: "There can be no *power over* without *power for,*" and the positive form of it is: "Treat human beings according to what they may become with the best available aid, and our own." The meaning of this principle can be inferred from a set of six propostions which he expressly denies. These are:

That western civilization must control the world, or perish;

That capital requires a market expanded by pressure regardless of the quality of the means used;

That the rate of expansion cannot be controlled;

That an honest and disinterested service to other states is impossible;

That the amount we charge for our services to peoples backward in any respect must always be the maximum obtainable;

That this charge must include political control.

And then he concludes with this statement: "What I assert is that, in all these matters the ethical question is pertinent, and ethical action within our power."[2]

An interesting doctrine in *The Spirit of World Politics* is Professor Hocking's theory that a people capable of self-government are better off under a poor government of their own than they would be under a good alien regime. He believes that it inhibits cultural creativity in a people to have their territory occupied by alien administrative officials be these civilians or military personnel. Thus Professor Hocking is the champion of the backward peoples of the earth against those who advocate and practice economic imperialism and exercise power over these people without ever even considering what is for their good. He has a strong conviction that a variety of virile and growing cultures upon the earth, each contributing to world civilization what the peculiar genius of that people will enable them to contribute, when they are allowed to make history in accordance with the hypothesis "of equal racial potency," is "the only possible basis for an expanding world intercourse." He is strongly opposed to standardization, and the reduction of the various living cultures of the earth to a uniform technological pattern. Let there be an intermingling of cultures, but let each express itself in accordance with its specific genius, in government, art, science and philosophy. This doctrine may be called cultural pluralism. Thus any satisfactory international arrangement to control atomic bombs and to regulate the relations between states to prevent the outbreak of another catastrophic war, must be general enough to leave the various peoples of the earth free to evolve and to make history in their own way. Such independent history-making and cultural creativity will greatly enrich human civilization as a whole.

A political philosophy such as Professor Hocking has pre-

---

[2] *The Spirit of World Politics*, p. 509.

sented in his various writings is open to attack on at least two counts. First, it can be charged with being too metaphysical and not sufficiently realistic. Along with this charge would go the complaint that he sticks too closely to tradition, and, in spite of a pretense at being liberal, is really defending a conservative viewpoint. And a second charge would be that he is not only too metaphysical in his own political thinking, but he is dominated by a bad German type of metaphysics which stems from Fichte and Hegel. Since we have now waged two terribly destructive world wars to put down a German state which its own defenders claimed was based upon the political philosophy founded by Fichte and Hegel, many British and American political theorists have denounced such a totalitarian state as an end in itself.

In answer to these charges it is only fair to say that Professor Hocking is neither a conservative nor a totalitarian in his political philosophy. He is a genuine progressive, seeking earnestly to minimize as much as possible the use of force, both within a state and between states, in order to bring about a condition of lasting domestic and world-wide peace and concord. For only in such an era of human history can the non-competitive cultural values be enhanced, and only through their enhancement can a better breed of human beings be developed.

Whether one likes Professor Hocking's political philosophy or not, it must be conceded that he has richly contributed to our American philosophical literature in the field of political thought. And personally I am convinced that his insistence that political philosophy has its beginning and its fulfillment in certain basic ethical postulates will abide as a permanent contribution to our conception of the democratic state, even though his special formulation of the various postulates may need to be changed.

X

HOCKING'S "EXPERIMENT IN EDUCATION"

Here is my review of Hocking's important book, *Experiment in Education,* which was published by Henry Regnery Company in 1954. It is reprinted from *Philosophy and Phenomenological Research,* Vol. XV, 1955, pp. 424-426. It is followed by Hocking's own extended clarifying comments on the book and its place in his writings.

Experiment in Education has as its subtitle "What We Can Learn from Teaching Germany." It is a timely and significant addition to Professor Hocking's excursive and descriptive works. He was in residence at the University of Leiden during the academic year 1947-48, and during the spring and early summer of 1948 he made an extensive tour of occupied Germany, and attended sessions of the War Crimes Court at Nuremberg. He studied in Germany in 1902 and 1903 and he toured the country in 1938.

One half of Professor Hocking's dedication of this book runs "To Germany immortal, in gratitude and sorrow, in love and faith." Although he does not prophesy as to what the future of "Germany immortal" may be, this dedicatory statement clearly indicates the spirit in which the author approaches the task of evaluating the work of our occupational forces which he suggests in the other half of the dedication: "To American knight errantry in education." Throughout the book one detects a certain nostalgia in the author for the Germany he knew as a student. Having now attained the eminence of dean among living American philosophers, his masterly analysis, evaluation, and indictment of our stupendous attempt to change the mentality of the German people after World War II deserves the careful attention of students of philosophy, international relations, political science, and the philosophy of education.

In Part One, "The Unique Enterprise," Professor Hocking gives a preliminary statement of the problem, and explains our conception of our mandate. He distinguishes the negative aspect of our task, "endeavoring to uproot and destroy any fragmentary momenta of the Hitler mentality that might be surviving," from the affirmative aspect, "replacing the Hitler outlook by a working German mentality which could fulfill the specification of the mandate as 'peace-loving'." (pp. 25f.)

Part Two deals with "The Negative Phase: Curing Hitlerism." After a preliminary statement of the problem, he devotes a long chapter (VI) to the effects of the defeat on the mentality of the German people, and to a study of the War Crimes Court. The author claims that we overworked punishment and retribution. He writes: "There *was* no victor's faith that change of heart was possible in the premises: the losers must taste deep and long the flavor of their sin; they were not to consider themselves liberated but conquered; our intention, in brief, was *punishment.*" (P. 41.) Professor Hocking's account of the Court is penetrating and informative, and is especially valuable for teachers and students of legal and ethical justice.

Three chapters in Part Two are concerned with "Denazification" (VI-VIII). In evaluating our efforts in this regard, Professor Hocking especially mentions four errors we made. These are: (1) "Our primary error was that of *measuring presumptive guilt by Party-connectedness and official rank,* a fallacy from which our German colleagues were prepared to save us, and tried to save us" (p. 93); (2) Our not knowing when to stop, our failure to make a distinction between exemplary retribution, and full and complete punishment of every party member; (3) Our "assumption of fixed guilt classes" (pp. 93ff.); and (4) "The creation of a festering pool of idle talent." (pp. 98f.) Yet we did these important things: "To the self-righting forces within Germany we gave effective aid. We furnished the stage-setting favorable to a recovered historical perspective; we removed the warping strain of police pressure upon all phases of life, upon free thinking and, by stages, upon the free expression of thought. We gave a provisional social and political set-up, with provision as well for its own internal change and growth. We brought to light many items of a suppressed true history of Germany itself during the Nazi period—data for German reflection to work upon. Meantime we kept Germany alive and in order. And we gave an element of hope and good will." (P. 106.)

Part Three deals with "The Affirmative Phase: Promoting Democracy." In Chapter IX the author clearly explains how we confused American democracy with "democracy in its root-principle," and teaching democracy with democratizing teaching. Our attempts to remake German education are discussed in Chapter X, and in Chapter XI he quotes at length from two provocative letters which he received from German students.

From the standpoint of metaphysics the most important section of the book is Part IV, "The Metaphysical Ground." It consists of a single chapter (XII,) entitled "Political Patience via Cosmic Patience." Here Professor Hocking states and defends the thesis: "The disorder of the human world is in its root a metaphysical disorder." (P. 159.) And what is this disorder in our world of the twentieth century? It is a universal impatience with all extant political, social, and religious institutions based upon the repudiation of a metaphysical or ontological justice that transcends all of these human institutions. This was Hitler's metaphysical blind-spot, and it is also the radical evil in naturalistic conceptions of democracy, as well as in Marxian socialism, the metaphysics of which is dialectical materialism. The cure for this disorder and for the impatience which is its root is the rediscovery of justice as an eternal ontological principle, because this idea is the only one that will enable modern men to carry the load of human creativity patiently. Professor Hocking lays down the principle dogmatically that we must "rediscover the scope of our own will," which is *"a will to create through suffering.* Here is the breeding place of a cosmic patience which in turn can beget political patience." (P. 163.)

Part Five, "Unfinished Business: The International Outlook" contains especially valuable contributions to political ethics, presented against the background of world politics between the two world wars. Chapter XIII includes interesting autobiographical data, mingled with significant interpretations of key events. Chapter XIV constitutes a useful supplement to the principles of political ethics set forth in the author's *Spirit of World Politics* and *Man and the State*. Here he deals with peace and proposes nine theorems of justice derived from the basic ethical principle, the "will to create through suffering," which was stated above.

Part Six, "Gains Achievable; Learnabilia" is of the utmost importance to those interested in a philosophy of education. Chapter XV, "Paradoxes of Moral Education" formulates six educational principles "we may learn from trying to teach Germany." In Chapter XVI, Professor Hocking exposes the fallacy that our emphasis on the social sciences was needed to correct the "backwardness of German schools in the field of social studies.'' He discusses four ''learnabilia on the supposed lacks of German universities in social studies.'' Chapter XVII is entitled ''The Ideal of Paucity: Essentials of General Education.'' Paucity, restricting the number of courses offered in the curriculum, has always been the German ideal and it is sharply contrasted with our American ideal ''of the greatest education for the greatest number,'' entailing an almost endless proliferation of courses, which is expounded in Chapter XVIII, entitled ''American Education Revisited.'' This chapter concludes with the formulation of six basic educational principles to clarify the meaning of the American democratic ideal of education.

Professor Hocking has written books that are more important philosophically than *Experiment in Education*, but he has never written one that is more timely. He does not presume to answer, but he throws a strong beam of light on the crucial question: Will the Soviet Union or the Free World of the West ultimately succeed in unifying and winning the German people? Consequently, this book deserves the thoughtful attention of all of those who are interested in and are concerned about the role the United States has been playing in Germany since the end of World War II.

XI

HOCKING'S LETTER AND COMMENTS ON "EXPERIMENT IN EDUCATION"

When I finished this review of *Experiment in Education* I sent it to Professor Hocking with the suggestion that he make whatever comments he wished to make on it. I received his reply with detailed important elucidations and explanations of why he wrote as he did. His letter was written at his home in Madison, New Hampshire, and is dated August 16th, 1954.

My dear Robinson:

I can't figure out how in the midst of a summer when by rights you should be vacationing, whereas in fact you are running summer courses and packing up for a year at Bethany College, you can still manage to do an exemplary review for an unreviewable book!

I say unreviewable as a considered judgment after noting that no real reviews have appeared. The reason dawns on me: the book is no one thing,—it is one thing and another, reminiscence, interpretation of history, comment on education, theory of law, international order, metaphysics. It is pluralistic: but is it a pluralistic universe?

You have my gratitude for the undertaking, and for what you have achieved, a remarkably substantial and just account of the amblying document. But you have done more: you have submitted your account to the author, a most generous proceeding, and as you know exceedingly perilous. I appreciate this generosity very highly, especially in this case of my ugly duckling; and I shall respond with friendly appreciation, the more so since you are the rare reviewer every author dreams of, one of his own ilk, to whom he can confide all the secrets of his composition. And in this case he can confess a certain trap set for his readers, and can offer the key to the riddle.

The trap is an ironical-parenthesis, or rather "ironically labelled" parenthesis. The parenthesis is chapter XII, presented as a "digression" which the reader may omit. It is the only chapter which is also a Part, all to itself. This may warn the suspicious reader that the author, after all, regards it as important. And if the reader is sleuth-minded he may note that it is introduced as a "digression into the heart of the subject," p. 150. Well, that is what it is: it is the philosophical substance of the book, whose burden, simply stated, is that Germany's aberration was metaphysical; that the deep suffering of our age, its loss of bearings, is metaphysical; that our errors in education, our failure to convey "democracy," so far as we did fail was metaphysical; that the weakness of our jurisprudence, and the incompetence of our struggle for a world order, are at bottom metaphysical; and that the cure for all of this must be metaphysical, namely a revision of Descartes and Kant (163, 289).

And having thus deliberately concealed my leaven, as the Gospel recommends, in "three measures of meal," it is my duty to my too-kind reviewer to unveil the obscured argument. I shall do this on a separate page. . . .

And further, since I am speaking to a friend and colleague, I feel not an "ought" but a "privilege" in putting on another sheet the placing of this odd, and apparently out-of-bounds document in the total plan of my terminal program of writing. . . .

Sincerely yours,
Signed: Ernest Hocking

To this letter Professor Hocking appended not one but two singlespaced sheets of highly significant additional comments about *Experiment in Education,* which should be carefully studied by every student who wants to understand the book.

Here are the contents of those two sheets just as he typed them at his home on that August day of 1954.

The philosophical aspect of the book (misleadingly) entitled *Experiment in Education.* (Note that the experiment is not discussed; but that its discussion turns on a brief epitome of a metaphysical outlook newly approached, and stated in shockingly simple terms.)

The metaphysical Chapter is addressed to "the whole philosophical craving of our time" (156) on the thesis that "the disorder of the world is at its root a metaphysical disorder." (159)

The analysis of the disorder is carried out as a development of Royce's "Our Finite Situation," and with reference to the Existentialist embroidery on the distresses of finitude, to Buddha, Kirkegaard, and the religious picture of the "lost soul."

This picture of human lostness is simplified and generalized as the situation of any human being who faces a world which is precisely what it appears to be to the naturalist eye, an unresponsive encounter with death. (157)

The Existentialist fumbling needs to be interpreted to itself, as (unawares) an unfinished Cartesianism of passion. (158) If the naturalist picture is right, Marx is right; religion is an opiate. And the practical corollary is metaphysical impatience in view of a world process devoid of justice, the essence of Nazism (160) on its metaphysical side.

The metaphysical issue of the time is thus restated (as at the same time a religious and a political issue) : can there be within the real a "justification for mass patience?"

The issue is momentarily set aside in its direct metaphysical character, in favor of an enquiry into the dialectic of pain, leading to the thesis that the "best of all possible worlds" could not possibly be a painless world, since the nature of love and of the "opening of the eyes to beauty" call for the service of pain. (162)

But the metaphysical issue is resumed (163) in the radical thesis that "the perceptions of love and of beauty ... are at the same time perceptions of the nature of "reality" a position here dogmatically stated. The dogmatism has its own appeal here on two counts (1) that the thesis is itself an account of (universal) experience, directly verifiable, and (2) that ultimate truth can best recommend itself in the simplest terms:* Argument must come, but it may come later. Meantime, there are other corroborations such as we find in Masefield, So Long to Learn, 180, etc., and in the capacity of this thesis to resolve the intricacies of contemporary philosophical tangles.

(Perhaps I should also say a word or two about the *placement of this essay* in the general program of my work).

This book is in one sense an *aside*. It is the product of a strong impulse to help those elements of a destroyed Germany in which the best hopes for the future lie, namely, the most sensitive and decent souls whom I found in '48 shattered by despair and shame.

In another sense, the book is a *necessary part* of my tight-set program of obligations-to-write, and would never have been done apart from that fact. First, because the German debacle is the concrete philosophical issue of our time, not to be dealt with by simply invoking the Declaration of Independence: if we evade

---

* Personally, I have long been reacting against complexity and metaphysics, such as I met early in Husserl, and later in Whitehead's categorical scheme; and moving toward a faith in simply-statable primary truths, which themselves invite dialectical structure of defense.

thinking it through afresh, we abandon the central spiritual
struggle. Second, because this book was a necessary preliminary to finishing the William James lectures at Harvard (developed at Leyden) on philosophy of law, which lectures are, in
turn, essential parts of the metaphysical scheme which is my
life work.

> For metaphysics has two aspects, logical and empirical.
> Its logical aspect is *a priori* and necessary, dialectical.
> Its empirical aspect, its footing in human experience, is
> in turn twofold: (a) The direct deliverance of self-
> awareness, now often called Existenz; (b) The induc-
> tions from ordered experience, such as law and economy
> and art. . . .

My excursive and descriptive works, such as *Morale and its
Enemies, Spirit of World Politics, Re-thinking Missions* . . . are
exercises in *inductive metaphysics*. This present book is another
such.

The right so to consider them rests on a logical thesis developed in the present book,—a paradoxical doctrine to the effect
that the work of induction leads to the revelation of *a priori,* as
its latest and most perfect achievement. (225-6, 228, 238, 288)

The ethical and political corollaries are the affirmation (in
view of the relativity of all relativities) of a moral absolute (288)
often referred to as "moral common sense" (103, etc.) ; and the
assertion, novel in juristic theory, that the concern for justice
is wider than the concern for law,—so that we must seek justice
in pre-legal issues. (208) Our teaching of "democracy" in Germany failed to touch this crucial point.

In short, this book may be described roughly as an empirical
contribution to an idealistic world-view. And my Gifford Lectures, if and when they come out, will maintain (under the general theme of Fact—the irrational particular—and Destiny) that
it is this empirical supplement to its dialectical argument that is
now chiefly needed to give an idealistic metaphysic a renewed
hold on the gropings of mankind. (Here end Hocking's comments on his own book.)

Experiment in Education was published in the author's eighty-
first year, and these extended comments and the letter to me
were penned at the beginning of his eighty-second year. Nevertheless this book will always be numbered among the major book-
length writings of Hocking.

XII

HOCKING'S CONCEPTION OF GOD

William Ernest Hocking (1878-1966) a student of Royce and James at Harvard University and later Alford Professor of Philosophy there, is generally recognized today as the leading representative of absolutistic personalism in the United States. More than any other American philosopher he has succeeded in synthesizing the empirical and the rational elements in religious thinking. In labeling his own theory he refers to it as "realism," "mysticism," and "idealism." Interpreting the first of these terms he calls his position "realism of social experience" and "social realism," and concerning the name idealism he insists that he holds a "realism of the Absolute, not far moved from Absolute idealism." He also says that his view is "a transfigured naturalism."

Hocking's *magnum opus* is entitled, *The Meaning of God in Human Experience* (1912), and the title suggests that God performs a special function in our experiences which will be explained presently. Since that monumental and now classic volume appeared, Hocking has published a number of other important works dealing in whole or in large part with the philosophy of religion. Among these should be mentioned: *Human Nature and its Remaking* (1918, new and revised edition 1923), *The Self—Its Body and Freedom* (1938), *Lasting Elements of Individualism* (1937), *Thoughts on Death and Life* (1937), *Living Religions and a World Faith* (1940), and *Science and the Idea of God* (1944). He was Gifford Lecturer at the University of Glasgow 1937-1939, and Hibbert Lecturer at Oxford and Cambridge Universities in 1938. Hocking has contributed numerous valuable articles to philosophical and religious journals. The philosophy of religion, metaphysically interpreted, has always been a field of major interest and concern to him. Being a first-rate thinker, gifted with a penetrating and original mind, his contributions to American philosophy of religion stand out as the most substantial that have been produced during the first half of the twentieth century.

The best approach to an understanding of Hocking's unique contribution to liberal philosophy of religion is through his solution of the problem of how we know other minds. His doctoral thesis at Harvard University dealt with this problem, and it contains the germs of the *Meaning of God in Human Experience.* Hocking went back to Fichte, who was the first philosopher seriously to raise the question of how we know other minds, and used that author's moral idealism as a foundation upon which he constructed an original religious metaphysics.

Each experiencer, Hocking contends, is continually confronted with two kinds of active outer realities—other experiencers who are like himself and who are in communication with him, and physical objects which beat in upon him in unnumbered and innumerable coercive sensory stimuli. At first the experiencer, misled by common sense realism, imagines that these two outer realms of being are entirely different, and he builds up complicated categories of physical nature and of social life on this unjustifiable assumption. But further reflection, coupled with intuitive insight, reveals another reality beyond physical nature and beyond the separate minds of our fellows, and we eventually discover that this transcendent but environing reality is a Being who can and does communicate with us. Hence that ultimate reality is Other Mind or God. Hocking concludes that this knowledge of Other Mind or God which all men possess, at least potentially, is the true explanation of how we know the minds of our fellows. If we think of this supreme Other Mind as the Absolute Personal God we will comprehend why this position is called absolutistic personalism in contrast with pluralistic personalism. Like Emerson, Hocking thinks that God is the spiritual supersolar blaze of light who gives us eyes to see, ears to hear, and minds to communicate with our fellows. This is the meaning of God in human experience that our relationship to him makes possible both the development of self-consciousness and of social consciousness neither of which is capable of independent reality.

In this short essay it is not possible to expound in any detail the elaborate arguments Hocking uses to establish this basic thesis. However, it is possible to state briefly his reconstruction of the classic ontological argument, which he considers to be far superior to the cosmological and teleological arguments for the existence of God. He writes: ''I have preferred to state the argument not thus: I have an idea of God, therefore God exists. But rather thus: I have an idea of God, therefore I have an experience of God. . . Insofar as reality dwells in Self, or Other Mind, or Nature, an ontological argument may be stated in proof of their existence. . . The object of certain knowledge has this threefold structure, Self, Nature, and Other Mind; and God the appropriate object of ontological proof, includes these three.''

God must be real because we have an experience of him in knowing the minds of our fellows. Brightman starts with the self as the primary datum. Hocking starts with God as the all-inclusive Being who unites self, other minds, and nature in a communal spiritual reality that is ineffable by the inductive method which yields valid scientific knowledge, but is known, in part at least, in the mystical experiences of saints and seers. Therefore, God is metaphysically real even though his essence surpasses our powers of comprehension. [1]

---

[1] See the informative essay by Arthur E. Luther: "W. E. Hocking on Man's Knowledge of God" in *Philosophy Today*, Vol. XI, pp. 131-141.

PART THREE

SELECTED LETTERS

XIII

HOERNLÉ'S LETTER ON ROYCE

The late R. F. A. Hoernlé (1880-1943), friend and former associate of Bernard Bosanquet at St. Andrews University, was a colleague of Josiah Royce on the faculty of the Department of Philosophy at Harvard University when Royce died. He wrote to Bosanquet who preserved the letter and it has been published in *Bernard Bosanquet and his Friends, Letters;* edited by J. H. Muirhead, George Allen and Unwin, London, 1935, Letter LXXXIV, pp. 188f. The letter was written on December 7, 1916. Note that Bosanquet states that these comments were sent to him by Hoernlé, and were probably written as an obituary notice.

Bernard Bosanquet

The Heath Cottage
Oxshott
Surrey
England

Josiah Royce died on September 14, 1916. The following lines, intended as an obituary notice, have been sent me by Professor Hoernlé, who doubts, however, whether this was ever published.

Owing to accidents of the post, which curtail the time at my disposal my words must be few if they are at all to reach their goal.

What I have admired, and what has inspired me, in the writings of Professor Royce, is the courage and high audacity with which he has carried forward the banner—I will not say of Idealism, that ambiguous term, but of a profound spiritual philosophy. I take as typical the sentence "As for me, I love the sea, and am minded to find in it life, and individuality, and explicit law." He has always decisively committed himself, and has confronted the most ultimate and arduous problems, with the same spirit and enthusiasm with which the most passionate votary of a great religion might enter upon the task of commending it to the world. Only Professor Royce's work has been done, as he may justly claim, not by the arts of the popular preacher, but by the lofty enterprise of the scholarly philosopher. What carries us with him is a lucidity born of his ardour not a facility born of unlaborious sentiment.

It would not be becoming for me to enter, in the brief minutes at my disposal, upon the precise nature of his contribution to the problems which concern the real and the individual. It is more fitting simply to acknowledge the debt which I owe to the study of his Gifford Lectures, and to say that my own much slighter efforts to find a footing in these same regions would probably never have taken definite form but for his leadership and example.

If we look back for half-a-century over the English-speaking world, we shall be amazed at the progress which during that interval the pursuit of philosophy has made within it. Philosophy no longer depends on one or two or three of the nations of Europe. It has put a girdle round about the earth, and has set itself beyond any dangers which might appear to menace the culture of that older world. It is partly for this reason, because in him and in such as him we see tokens that the future of the human spirit is secure, that especially in this terrible year we rejoice to pay our homage to the high and many sided genius of Josiah Royce.[1]

---

[1] My doctors dissertation, *The Place of Inference in Logical Theory*, was done under the direction of Professor Hoernlé. I edited, with a *Memoir*, his *Studies in Philosophy* (George Allen & Unwin Ltd., London) & (Harvard University Press, 1952). In addition to this posthumously published collection of his essays his major philosophical works are:

Studies in Contemporary Metaphysics (Harcourt, Brace & Co., 1920); *Matter, Life, Mind, and God*, (Harcourt, Brace & Co., 1923); *Idealism as a Philosophical Doctrine* (Hodder & Stoughton, 1924). This book was revised and enlarged and the title changed to *Idealism as a Philosophy* (George H. Doran Company, 1927). See also his important article "Solipsism" in Hastings' *Encyclopedia of Religion and Ethics*.

Two other valuable books by Professor Hoernlé were published at the University of Witwatersrand, Johannesburg, South Africa, where he was Professor during the last years of his life. They are: *South African Policy and the Liberal Spirit*, 1939, and *Race and Reason: Selected Contributions*, edited with a *Memoir* by Professor I. D. MacCrone, 1945.

XIV

JOSIAH ROYCE'S LETTERS TO
WILLIAM TORREY HARRIS

William Torrey Harris was the founder and leading representative of the St. Louis School of Philosophy, which was so strongly Hegelian that he has been called "the leading American proponent of Hegel" and "our foremost American Hegelian." I served as Chairman of the Harris Centennial Committee of the Western Division of the American Philosophical Association to plan a Centennial Year Program in honor of Dr. Harris. The thirty-sixth Annual meeting of the Division was held in St. Louis in 1935. The addresses honoring Dr. Harris that were given at this meeting were published by the Open Court Publishing Company in 1936 under the editorship of Edward L. Schaub, with the title *William Torrey Harris 1835-1935*. Dr. Kurt F. Leidecker addressed the meeting on "Harris and Indian Philosophy," and he prepared an excellent bibliography for the memorial Volume titled "Bibliography: William Torrey Harris in Literature." The most complete biography of Dr. Harris is Dr. Leidecker's *Yankee Teacher—The Life of William Torrey Harris,* (Philosophical Library, 1946).

Miss Edith Davidson Harris, daughter of William Torrey Harris, has presented to the Hoose Library of the School of Philosophy of the University of Southern California a number of important letters that were written to her father while he was Editor and Publisher of *The Journal of Speculative Philosophy,* and continuing through the period that he served as U. S. Commissioner of Education. Among this collection of letters are those written by Josiah Royce.

The year 1955 being the Centenary of the birth of Josiah Royce, he having been born in Grass Valley, California on November 20th, 1855, these letters were first published in *The Philosophical Forum,* (Vol. XIII, 1955, Boston University), to commemorate the occasion. Facsimiles of President Gilman's letter to Harris, and of Royce's first letter and the postcard are reproduced in my edition of *Royce's Logical Essays* (pp. vi-x). With this exception these letters of Royce to Harris had never before been published. They are now reprinted here because of their biographical importance.

While Royce was a graduate student at Johns Hopkins University, he prepared a paper entitled *The Ethical Studies of Schiller* for presentation to the Johns Hopkins Philological Association. It is interesting to note that this paper was completed near Royce's twenty-second birthday, since his first letter to Harris was written on January 4, 1878. He received the Ph.D. Degree in philosophy at Johns Hopkins University in June of 1878. He was appointed Instructor in English at the University of California and went there to teach in August before his twenty-third birthday in November.

Royce was advised by President Gilman to offer his paper on Schiller to Harris for publication in the *Journal of Speculative Philosophy*. He sent the paper by express and addressed his first letter to Harris as follows:

> Johns Hopkins University
> Baltimore, Md.
> Jan. 4, 1877 ('78)

Mr. W. T. Harris,
   Dear Sir:
   I send by express to your address this day a transcript of an essay of my own on "The Ethical Studies of Schiller." The essay was read before the Johns Hopkins Philological Association; and at Pres. Gilman's advice I take the liberty of asking you if you can make any use of the manuscript for the "Journal of Speculative Philosophy." The subject is of course no new one; yet so far as I know there is no very extensive literature in English treating of it. In any case, Kant's influence on German Literature is a topic, it seems to me, that would bear much discussion. If you would encourage the idea, I should like also at some future time, to offer an essay on the philosophic studies of Novalis, in which I should seek to discuss Kant's influence on the early Romanticists.
   I hope I do not trespass upon your time too much in thus addressing myself to you without having had the pleasure of a previous introduction. After all it may not be unwelcome to you to

hear a word of the philosophic studies that a few at the Johns Hopkins University are engaged in; even though you may not find much worth in what I herewith send.

Believe me Sir,

Very Respectfully
Yours Truly,

Signed: Josiah Royce,
Fellow in Philosophy
J. H. U.

We do not know what Harris wrote in reply to this letter, but we have positive proof that Royce visited Harris in St. Louis the following August and discussed with him the publication of this his first published philosophical essay. This proof is found in two letters in the Royce-Gilman collection at the Library of Johns Hopkins University. I am indebted to Professor Max Fisch of the University of Illinois for lending me his copies of these letters. On July 16, 1878, Royce addressed a letter to President Gilman, who was then vacationing in Amherst, Massachusetts, about his prospective journey west to begin his work as Instructor in English at the University of California. In this letter, he wrote: "I want to go through St. Louis, and in particular to meet Harris. I should be much obliged if you could find it convenient to give me a letter of introduction to him. I think some acquaintance with him might be of advantage to me."

President Gilman at once wrote the following letter of introduction to Harris:

Dr. Wm. T. Harris
My dear Sir:
Allow me to introduce to you Mr. Josiah Royce who has been in the Johns Hopkins University for two years as a graduate student of Philosophy and Literature and is now called to his alma mater as Assistant Professor in the University of California. You will quickly discover his interest in and acquaintance with philosophical thought and perhaps you will enlist him as an occasional writer for your excellent Journal. I commend him in a special manner to your confidence and regard.

Yours with high Esteem,
D. C. Gilman
Amherst, Mass.
July 18, 1878

103 Irving St.

Cambridge, Mass.

April 20, 1894.

Dear Dr. Harris: —

I will con=
sent to read a paper, in response
to the report of the committee,
on the Psychology of the Imitative
Functions in its relation to the
process of learning, on July 9,
the day that you choose from
among the days in question.

Only I shall need, I presume, ample notice of the contents of the Committee's report, as I shall prefer to prepare and read a paper, and do not want to leave my remarks to the chances of extempore speech. I assume then that I shall get such notice in due time

Yours Very Truly
Josiah Royce.

After he had settled in Berkeley, Royce wrote Gilman a report of his journey. In this letter, dated Monday, September 16, 1878, from Berkeley, Alameda, California, Royce wrote: "I received a note from Harris the other day, promising me that my Schiller article shall appear in his October number. I met him in St. Louis as I passed through, and have to thank you for a very interesting interview obtained through your introduction. I shall make further efforts towards publication soon."

Royce received a copy of advanced sheets of the Journal containing his article in Berkeley about the middle of October, 1878. We know this from a postcard which Royce mailed to Harris on October 23rd. It contains a request that a typographical error be corrected, and Harris made the correction in the *Errata* of the next number of the Journal, Vol. XII, p. iv. Here is Royce's postcard:

San Francisco
Oct. 23, 1878

Dear Sir:

The advance sheets of the Journal have been received. I had a single Latin phrase in the article: "Solvitur ambulando." My copyist or the printer has made it *sobriatur* ambulando. Would it be possible for you to have noted in the supplement of the Journal this error. Otherwise the nonsense seems too glaring. But the matter is of little consequence. I should like to purchase 30 copies of this number of the Journal, and have them forwarded by Exp. C. O. D.

Excuse haste—Yours,
J. Royce

With regard to Royce's expression in his first letter to Harris of his desire to write at some future time "an essay of the philosophic studies of Novalis," attention is called to sections II and III of Lecture VI of *The Spirit of Modern Philosophy*. In section II Royce mentions Novalis whose real name was Friedrich V. Hardenberg. He there writes: "Novalis, who died very young, touches, in his fragmentary remains, upon all the characteristic interests of the romanticists; he is philosophical, poetical, critical; but he is everywhere and always the born dreamer." And in section III Royce gives a penetrating and sympathetic exposition of the philosophy of Novalis, whom he considered especially typical of German romanticism. This lecture, then, is the final fulfillment of the desire expressed in his first letter to Harris.

Royce's second letter to Harris contains an exceptionally interesting explanation of his failure to write for the *Journal of Speculative Philosophy* an article on the philosophy of Shadworth Hodgson. We do not have Harris's reply, but presumably and so far as the writer knows Royce never did get around to writing this article. However, Harris did accept for publication the Kant Centennial essay entitled "Kant's Relation to Modern Philosophical Progress," which Royce must have had Professor Mears forward to Harris after it was read for him at the Kant Centennial at Saratoga, New York, on July 6th, he being unable to attend. Here is Royce's second letter:

Berkeley, Aug. 23, 1881

Dr. Wm. T. Harris:
Dear Sir:
I am informed by Professor Mears that you now have in your hands the MS of an essay that I wrote for the "Kant Centennial." I should be glad to know whether you can find a place for it in the *Journal*. I desire however as well to offer you an explanation and apology for my failure to fulfill my old promise of the summer of 1878 to write you a notice of Shadworth Hodgson.

I have borne my promise in mind ever since, but have never felt sure of my ability to fulfill it. Hodgson seems to me an author difficult not so much in his own thought, though that is often obscure, as in view of his curious historical position. One needs a fair understanding of his doctrine before one feels able to judge of its importance; so numerous and subtle, not to say heterogeneous, seem his relations to other modern tendencies. My lack of historical comprehension of Hodgson has therefore stared me in the face whenever I have tried to begin my essay, which I have therefore constantly delayed until some one more book should be read or piece of work done. I can, now I think, undertake the work quite soon, and finish it. But perhaps you no longer desire such a contribution from me. A word of advice on the subject would be very welcome. I regret having been, or rather having seemed so neglectful.

One other matter I must mention. The extra Nos. you sent me of the *Journal* for Oct. '78, containing my article on *Schiller*, were to be $3.75. I asked that they should be sent C.O.D. My express bill was $5.50, which I took to include the express charges and the original bill. If I was mistaken I am still owing you the old bill, and should be glad to know the fact if your books still show it. I have been constantly on the point of writing to you ever since, but have delayed, hoping to send the Hodgson article.

Very Respectfully
Yours Truly,
Josiah Royce

Royce's third letter to Harris acknowledges receipt of the page proof of his article on Kant, and calls Harris' attention to Hans Vaihinger's *Kant-Commentary*, which he offered to review for the *Journal of Speculative Philosophy*.

Berkeley, Alameda Co.,
Cal.
Dec. 28, 1881

Dr. W. T. Harris:
Dear Sir:

I thank you for the page proof of my article. I have seen no errors in the print. I shall be glad of 50 copies of the article separately printed. This time I will positively pay whatever they cost; but please forward them *by mail,* as express charges are enormous.

The Kant-year seems to have been quite productive. I have just bought a copy of Dr. Sterling's *text-book of Kant.* I have not had time to master it as yet, but I doubt not that it will turn out to be as enlivening and as thorough as any of his works.

If you have not already engaged some one for the purpose, I should like to have the privilege of writing a somewhat extended note (of four or five pages) for your Journal, on Hans Vaihinger's new *Kant-Commentary.* I have as yet seen no extended review of the book, but when it comes to me from my book-seller I intend to make a careful examination of it and to prepare a book-review. I could have one ready for your April number.

Yours truly
Josiah Royce

This letter was followed shortly by a brief note with which Royce enclosed payment for the *Journal.*

Berkeley, Feb. 3, '82.

Dear Sir:

I enclose $5 for the journals. They have not yet appeared, but I have the money in hand now and am unwilling to delay.

Yours Very Truly,
J. Royce

Ten years later Royce replied to Harris' request that he do something for Humphreys. This letter is of special interest because of the statement it contains about Hegel's *Phänomenologie*. Although the book Royce mentions was never published, his translation of the chapter entitled *The Contrite Consciousness* was included by Benjamin Rand in *The Modern Classical Philosophers,* and by Professor Jacob Loewenberg in *Hegel Selections,* and there is a long footnote which explains Hegel's "novel sort of Introduction to Philosophy."

103 Irving Street
Cambridge, Mass.
Dec. 4, 1892

Dear Mr. Harris:

I will try to do what I can for Humphreys.

My expected book is to be made up of translated extracts from the *Phänomenologie,* with introduction and notes. I am an admirer of that book, and mean to do what I can to make others feel the beauty of its analyses, whose value is by no means conditioned upon an acceptance of Hegel as a whole, or upon any theory as to his progress in his later works.

Yours Very Truly,
Josiah Royce

Royce's final three letters to Harris contain his acceptance of an invitation to address the National Council of Education on July 9th, 1894, his suggestions as to how the subject assigned by Harris should be modified so as to eliminate the word *hypnotic* from the title, and his request for help from the Bureau in assembling material for the address. These letters reveal Royce's deep interest in the problems of educational psychology and child study, and his squeamishness about discussing hypnotism in a public lecture.

103 Irving Street
Cambridge, Mass.
April 15, 1894

Dear Mr. Harris:

Your kind offer, in your letter of April 13, to assign to me a place for a report on the "Relation of Hypnotic Suggestion to the Process of Learning," at the meeting of the National Council of Education, July 9, is at hand, and I find myself much attracted by the proposed task. But I confess that, if you will permit me to make a suggestion, the topic as proposed could be a little altered in such a manner as to make a discussion of it still more profitable, in case my opinion is not at fault. The analogy between hypnotic suggestion and the process of learning is doubtless, as I tried to point out in the lecture to which you refer, a real analogy. But I suspect that a discussion limited in form to this analogy, would be likely to prove to many rather vague. The real point of the analogy would be brought out better if one made the topic: "The Psychology of the Imitative Functions in Childhood as related to the Process of Learning." If this topic could be the one chosen, I should be willing to take part, and would then be able to call attention to certain lines of "Child Study" that, as I think, can be profitably pursued in this connection. I might refer to the matter of the hypnotic analogy; but I confess that I do not want to discuss any topic in public on such an occasion if the *name* hypnotism is made too prominent in the title. The thing is interesting; the name is a little sensational in seeming. Besides "Imitation" names the really interesting topic. —Do you assent to such a change?

Yrs. Truly
J. Royce

103 Irving Street
Cambridge, Mass.
April 20, 1894

Dear Dr. Harris:

I will consent to read a paper, in response to the report of the committee, on the Psychology of the Imitative Functions in its relation to the process of learning, on July 9, the day that you choose from among the days in question. Only I shall need, I presume, ample notice of the contents of the Committee's report, as I shall prefer to prepare and read a paper, and do not want to leave my remarks to the chance of *extempore* speech. I assume then that I shall get such notice in due time.

Yours Very Truly
Josiah Royce

103 Irving Street
Cambridge, Mass.
May 13, 1894

Dear Dr. Harris:

I thank you for your kind encouragement. I will read at the Nat'l Educational Assoc'n when and how you want. But just now it is *facts* that I need, and I beg that, so far as there is the least chance, I may have the advice of your Bureau as to where and how to collect such facts—facts on all possible forms of imitativeness & of its apparent opposites when these exist. Can you suggest any further way to drum up facts? Wide range of comparison helps, in such matters, to correct the necessary defects of nonexpert observation. It is but a preliminary comparative survey of the field that I am now busy with.

Yours Very Truly
Josiah Royce

Royce had a keen sense of humor. This is evidenced by the fact that he enclosed in one of his letters to Harris a set of definitions under the caption "Extracts from a Vocabulary of Terms in Use at Clark University." These definitions are written in Royce's handwriting on his letter-head, 103 Irving Street, Cambridge, but they are undated and unsigned. Whether he composed them himself or collected them from his Harvard Colleagues, or from some other source can only be surmised. Here is the list of definitions as written by Royce:

Extracts from "A Vocabulary of Terms in Use
at Clark University."

Faculty — See s. v. *Resignation.*

Founder — A person who economizes his resources and lives to a surprising age.

Future — The time to which all significant questions and investigations should be postponed.

Literature of the Subject — A collection of titles of works that have not been consulted by the authors of psychological papers.

Pedagogy — The Art of keeping one's views and opinions dark, and of confusing the minds of inquiring persons.

Philosophy — A collection of speculations in which only the President of the University may indulge, and for which he declines to be held responsible.

President — A person of universal information; and adept in the Art of Pedagogy (q. v.); an officer to whom the faculty are accustomed to tender their Resignations.

Psychology — The Science of the Knee-Jerk and of related phenomena. N. B. ALL phenomena are related.

Religion — A sentiment of reverence and acquiescence in some consensus concerning fundamental questions. N.B. Religion includes nothing within the limits of any creed or cult.

Resignation — (1) The principal official act of the members of the Faculty. (2) The proper state of mind for one about to read any sentence of over ten lines in length in the published papers of the President.

Reverence — A state of mind to which one may safely confess if he is careful to say nothing about the nature of its object.

Seminary — (1) A collection of persons who do not understand one another's views. (2) A publication of the University whose proofs are never corrected.

University — An institution where Reaction-Times are tabulated.

These definitions were aimed at G. Stanley Hall, who was the Founder and President of Clark University. He had the reputation for coining new technical terms. At Harvard it used to be said that the graduate student, desirous of knowing what was meant by one of these new terms in Hall's writings, should not consult a dictionary, but should call the author on the telephone and ask him! Presumably no one else could possibly know what he meant.

I sent a reprint of these letters to Professor Hocking, and this elicited the following comments from him in a letter from Madison, New Hampshire, dated 20 March, 1960.

"I am especially interested . . . in Royce's Letters to Harris. Richard Hocking happens to be here at the moment, and I have copied off for him, at his request, the Extracts from Royce's waggish Vocabulary for Clark. That side of Royce is too little felt. You recall his reaction to the Eusapia Palladino episode in which Münsterberg detected the medium in using a foot to produce phenomena. Royce said:

> Eeny, meeny, miny, mo,
> Catch Eusapia by the toe;
> If she hollers, then you know
> James' doctrines are not so."

XV

TWO OTHER LETTERS OF JOSIAH ROYCE

Fortunately I have in my possession one other biographically significant letter of Josiah Royce, and an exact copy of another one, both of which I am inserting here.

Letter I

Among the many honors that were conferred on Josiah Royce, one that he highly valued was his election to corresponding membership in the Aristotelian Society of England. This letter is his thanks for and acceptance of that honor.

> 103 Irving Street,
> Cambridge, Mass.
> April 26, 1913

Mr. H. Wildon Carr,
Honorary Secretary of the Aristotelian Society.

My dear Professor Carr:
I accept with great pleasure the kind invitation of the Aristotelian Society to become a corresponding member.
If ever I can be of service to the Society, I shall be glad to do what is in my power. I am grateful for the honor conferred, and I hope, in future, to be able occasionally, when I visit England, to find the Society in session, and to attend its meetings.

> Very truly yours
> Signed: Josiah Royce

Letter II

This is a copy of a manuscript letter from Josiah Royce to the mother of Professor Jared Sparks Moore, during the graduate student days of the latter at Harvard University. The original letter was given to Professor Edgar S. Brightman by Professor Moore's widow, and he gave me a copy. Professor Moore was

Chairman of the Department of Philosophy at Western Reserve University for several years.

This letter is a good example of the kind of considerate opinion Royce had of his most promising graduate students.

> 103 Irving Street
> Cambridge, Mass.
> May 3, 1904

Dear Mrs. Moore:

I feel distinctly encouraged, as to your son's general prospects as a student and as a possible teacher of philosophy, in view of the account that I obtained from him this morning. His record, and what I already know of his work, were, as you know, favorably viewed by me before this talk. My favorable impression is rather strengthened by our discussion.

He has come to philosophy in a wholesome and natural way. He has made good use of his time so far. His present difficulty in making his thoughts intelligible to other people is due, not I think, to any fundamental defect of clearness in his thinking, but to the way in which he has read himself into certain aspects of his subject, to the exclusion of certain other aspects which he will in time learn to emphasize. His mental development, so far as philosophy is concerned, has been a little too solitary and independent. He needs practice in teaching, in discussion, etc. But there seems to be no trait in him that forbids him to get such practice as time goes on. I looked (as we talked together) for the various more or less defective, or if you choose, morbid motives that sometimes are present in young men who are driven into philosophy by a false or unfortunate sort of reflectiveness. I could find no sign of such motives in him. His philosophizing seems so far to be a natural and sensible enough process, imperfect as is still his power to convey to other people what he means. His religious experience seems to have been of a normal enough type, whatever you may think of the outcome,—an outcome with which I myself do not agree, although I have learned to respect strongly the motives which I have several times seen leading young people in the direction that he has followed, and that has led him into his present church connection. On that side he seems to me to be growing safely enough.

He has considerable independence and productiveness of thought, a pretty large power for work, a knowledge of what scholarship is, a high ideal, a healthy mind, and a good deal of learning. He ought to have paid more attention than he has done to natural science, and would have done well to study more mathematics, and also psychology. But there is time to make up for such incompletenesses.

I think that he ought to try to get a job of tutoring during the coming summer, so as to earn something. I should be glad to see him study here next year, and should think it justifiable to make considerable sacrifices to let him do so. Whether we could find a place for him as Assistant I cannot yet say. In any case he can make better use of his time here than elsewhere next year, so far as I can see.

It looks to me as if he would develop somewhat slowly, but very healthily, as a student and teacher of philosophy, and as if that were likely to be a good career for him.

His temperament,—cheerful on the whole, but not exactly sanguine,—unaggressive, but persistent,—seems to be favorable to a reasonable success. His health, as you all say, seems very good; but I should be glad to know that he exercised,—moderately, but regularly,—enough to ensure his always retaining, during his years of trial, his present soundness. He will have to study hard. He needs therefore all possible physical soundness.

My practical result is that you would do well, even at considerable cost to your patience, to let him go on developing in his present way, hoping, as I hope, that before too long a time he can be on his own feet as a professional man.

Yours Very Truly
Signed: Josiah Royce

As I read over my letter, I feel of course how fallible my judgment has to be. I can only report what so far I seem to see. I have done my best with the imperfect data so far accessible to me.

XVI

FOUR LETTERS OF STEPHEN ROYCE

Stephen Royce (A.B. Harvard, 1910), elder son of Josiah Royce, was highly intelligent. He knew a great deal about what his father was doing and was proud of his standing as a scholar and his achievements as a philosopher. Stephen Royce died June 12, 1954. I at once wrote Professor Hocking who replied in a letter dated August 16, 1954: "I am sorry to hear of Stephen Royce's death. It is a great bit of good fortune, for Royce's memory and influence, that you and Professor Cotton have gathered from him so much of biographical and intrinsic interest about Royce. Mrs. Royce was very reluctant to give out what she knew, on the ground that Royce himself had said of his Philadelphia address that it contained all that he wanted to say of his life's story."

I have never seen the letters Stephen Royce wrote to Professor Harry Cotton to which Hocking here refers. But I have carefully kept all of his letters to me. They are so informative and interesting that I have selected four of them for inclusion here.

Letter I

Letter I was not addressed to me, but to the India Academy of America, 200 West 57th Street, New York City, New York. It was dated February 6th, 1942. Stephen Royce sent it to me about eight years later with the notation: "Returned 2/11/42 marked 'Not at address given' and 'Not in directory'" Signed S. R. The famous astronomer to whom Stephen Royce refers in this letter was Simon Newcomb (1835-1909). He was rear admiral and professor at the United States Naval Observatory, was in charge of the office of the *Nautical Almanac,* and was editor of the *American Journal of Mathematics* for many years. See his biography in the 14th Edition of the *Encyclopedia Britannica.*

This letter is of the utmost importance for four reasons. (1) It contains an authoritative account of the source of Royce's knowledge of Hindu philosophy, with special reference to the discussions found in *The World and the Individual*. (Vol. I, pp. 78, 100-110, 156-165, 169-175, and 195) (2) This letter records the facts about the lifelong friendship between the distinguished orientalist and Sanskrit scholar, Charles Rockwell Lanman and Royce, with the fascinating story of the joke Lanman perpetrated on Royce in his own home to the enjoyment of Royce and the members of his family. This proves that he could take a joke even on himself. (3) This letter concludes with a statement about Münsterberg, who before World War I was a colleague and close friend of Royce, but who turned into a bitter enemy, at least in Royce's mind, when he became convinced that Münsterberg had, throughout his career on the faculty of Harvard University, been a paid agent of the German government. The tension and emotional strain of this experience was partly the cause of Royce's death September 14, 1916, at age sixty. Münsterberg died December 16, 1916, at age fifty-three. Letter II, written to me eight years later, also deals with the Münsterberg affair in greater detail. (4) This letter confirms the fact that in his later years Royce "did a great deal of long and laborious work on symbolic logic."

The Mr. Leidecker, to whom Stephen Royce refers in the opening sentence of this letter has been my friend for over thirty years. Dr. Kurt F. Leidecker is now Professor of Philosophy at Mary Washington College, Fredericksburg, Virginia. Born and reared to adulthood in Germany, he immigrated to the United States shortly after World War I. He received the A.B. degree from Oberlin College and the Ph.D. degree from the University of Chicago. As was indicated above, he is an authority on American Hegelian literature. His doctor's dissertation was in the field of oriental philosophy. He reads Pali and Sanskrit and is an authority on classical Hindu and Buddhist philosophical literature and sacred writings. Currently he is active in the Washington, D. C, area among persons interested in Hinduism and Buddhism.

I sent a copy of this letter of Stephen Royce to Professor Leidecker, and asked him whether he had ever seen it. He replied in a letter dated September 13, 1967, that he had received a copy and had filed it without answering it, in the hope that a second edition of his essay "Josiah Royce and Indian Thought" might in time be brought out but he added, "that time has not arrived."

He gave the following account of the Indian Society of America:

"The India Academy of America, with Professor John L. Gerig of Columbia as President, was an Institute of Cultural Cooperation incorporated under the laws of the State of New York and organized for the purpose of promoting exchange of intellectual and cultural influences between the United States and India. It superseded in 1930 the International School of Vedic and Allied Research whose headquarters were in New York City (the old Times Building), with Professor Charles Rockwell Lanman President of the American Section, the Marquess of Zetland President of the British Section, M. R. Jayakar President of the All-India Committee, and Pandit Jagadish Chandra Chatterji Director. The India Academy of America ceased to operate about 1932-33 when hit by the great depression of those years."

Regarding Josiah Royce's knowledge of Indian Philosophy, Professor Leidecker writes:

"Despite several inaccuracies and misinterpretations on the part of Royce of Indian concepts he must be given credit for having called attention to the Indian world of thought and its deep significance. He made it clear that it cannot be passed over lightly, that it had some relevance to western religious thinking. Above all he educated the intellectuals among the Christian laity to an appreciation of another realm of religious and philosophical thought not usually studied by them. In a sense, then, he continued the work so heroically begun by Emerson and Thoreau."

February 6th, 1942

India Academy of America,
200 West 57th Street,
New York City, New York.

Gentlemen:

The paper by Mr. Kurt Leidecker, then secretary of your academy, published in 1931, describing the relation of Josiah Royce's philosophy to Indic religious and philosophical thought, has just happened to be brought to my attention. Josiah Royce was my father.

The article in question goes to considerable effort to trace the source, extent, and date of my fathers's contact and interest in Indic thought, and bases this research entirely on analysis of the text of his various writings at different periods. The conclusion is reached that his philosophy is somewhat influenced by Indic thought, but indicates that he has little acquaintance with modern India and with modern Indic writings. The true source of his acquaintanceship with the Indic philosophers and theologians is in fact mentioned, but only incidentally, and the whole article leaves the source and extent of his Indian philosophical knowledge and contacts a mystery.

It has occurred to the writer that you might like to have this mystery cleared up. Incidentally, as my letterhead tells you, I am not a philosopher, and my knowledge of the subject is purely incidental from years of contact and conversation with my father in a purely informal way.

In briefly considering his life, Dr. Leidecker searches for, and is unable to find, the source of Josiah Royce's contact with Indic philosophy, and speculates that it was derived indirectly and incidentally through his familiarity with Schopenhauer, derived largely during his German studies.

What you have overlooked is the fact that Josiah Royce was one of the original group of Teaching Fellows who were called to the Johns Hopkins University at the time of its foundation in the late '70's. This group nearly all became outstandingly famous in their lines. It included my father, William James (loaned by Harvard), Edwin H. Hall, the physicist, and various other men who became outstanding scholars and scientists in the latter nineteenth century. Among these was Charles R. Lanman, the well-known Sanskrit scholar. He and my father and Professor Hall often talked of the first year at Johns Hopkins when there were almost no students, and the new faculty put in all their time teaching one another. It was at Johns Hopkins that Josiah Royce got his Ph.D. (Also LL.D. much later*)

He and Lanman were close neighbors and friends throughout his Harvard career, Lanman coming to Harvard from Johns Hopkins, and my father coming there after a brief return to the University of California, where he taught English Literature.

It was the Johns Hopkins period that put the finishing touches on the real breadth of my father's education. He had contact with Remsen, the chemist; with a famous astronomer, whose name at the moment escapes me; with Hall in physics; with a well-known Hebrew scholar; and with Lanman; among others. He and Lanman also had had contact already in Germany, but it

---

*He had LL.D.'s from Aberdeen, Lake Forest, Johns Hopkins, California, Harvard, Yale, Oxford, etc.

was the Johns Hopkins contact with Lanman which was most important.

Lanman at that time undertook to teach my father Sanskrit, and my father undertook to teach Lanman philosophy. The result was my father's knowledge of the Indic philosophers, and Lanman's beautiful translations of their writings. The interest of both men was, of course, primarily in classical India, rather than in modern India, just as the interest of both men was in classical Greece—its philosophy and language—rather than in modern Greece. Lanman developed increasing Indian contacts throughout his life, but they were mainly with Indian scholars whose interest was in classical Indic writings.

During the Johns Hopkins period, my father learned sufficient Sanskrit to read rather fluently, but he did not keep up this familiarity, though he constantly maintained the relation with Lanman during the many years that Lanman worked on the translations of Indic philosophical and theological writings. They were, like most of their Johns Hopkins group, extremely close friends for life, and maintained to their later years much of the youthful habit of deriding one another's best work in a spirit of the pleasantest kind of comradeship.

One particular incident might amuse you. My father had just published a book, which I believe was "The World and the Individual." The book was hardly off the press before Lanman came over with a very learned and entirely spurious writing of a non-existent ancient Indic philosopher, which writing he allegedly just had found. He had written a brief monograph on the subject in which he gave passages of the alleged original Sanskrit, with his learned translation thereof, containing numerous footnotes and alternative interpretations and text criticisms. The whole manuscript was a marvel of neatness, and was scholarly to the last degree. This Apocryphal Indic sage displayed in exaggerated form all of my father's habits of writing and of thought in the form of a caricature that was excruciatingly funny both to my father and to his entire family. Lanman reported that he had finally run down the real source of my father's entire philosophy and writings, and that before publishing my father's plagiarism to the world, the least he could do, in view of their long friendship, was to show him the article that he was going to publish. One particular passage of the translation still remains in my head, although I was only about twelve at the time this took place. In describing life, this counterfeit Indic sage made the following statement:

> "It seems that life is as a toad, which sitteth in the road; that if one steppeth neither on the toad nor on the road, the thing were done."

It sounds learned and rather mystic, a bit impossible, and just a trifle squishy; but as a fact, there was some passage which my father at once found in his own book which rather echoed the same sentiment.

This incident is just related for the amusement it may give and as an illustration of the close friendship of the two men and of their mutual interest and contact in Sanskrit, and in their common knowledge of the Indic philosophers.

It is a matter of regret to the writer that he is not sufficiently trained in philosophy to talk intelligently on more technical phases thereof. It may possibly interest you, however, to know that my father not only grew up in the mining camp of Grass Valley, California, but that he studied mining engineering at the University of California. The sole reason for his going into philosophy was that his baccalaureate address, at the time of his graduation from the University of California, was written on a subject involving the relation of Aeschylus' Prometheus Bound to the current Greek religion and mythology of its date. This address, based entirely upon independent study at the University library, in an institution where philosophy was not taught, so impressed a group of Berkeley and San Francisco businessmen that they put together a loan fund to send him to Germany to study. On his way there, he stopped at Boston and established contact with James and Palmer, and through them and the later Johns Hopkins association and studies, with a strong foundation of philosophic study in Germany, his philosophical career developed. He came to Harvard for a single year, to replace James during his Sabbatical year. The department was then enlarged to include him, and he taught at Harvard some 36 years.

He has several times told me that had it not been for that baccalaureate address and those clear-sighted businessmen, whom he had never seen in his life before, he would probably have been in my profession rather than in philosophy.

Needless to say, it is a matter of pleasure to the writer that from time to time philosophical people continue to show interest in my father's work.

I hope that this letter may be of some slight interest in clearing up what appeared to be rather a mystery to Dr. Leidecker, a mystery upon which he spent considerable time and effort. My impression from my father has always been that his philosophy, insofar as it was not strictly his own creation, descended from the Greek through various German schools of philosophical thought. It was my impression that little, if anything, in his philosophy could be said to derive from Indic sources. He was keenly interested in comparing these philosophies with his own and with other schools of thought. His early field of teaching at Harvard was the history of philosophy, and naturally he felt that the Indic philosophers belonged to this general historic picture, and therefore studied them with his life-long friend, Lanman. In later years, the history of philosophy became a lesser interest, and he was more interested in developing his own philosophy, and especially in developing the idealistic school of ethics, which is expounded especially in "The Philosophy of Loyalty" and "The Problem of Christianity."

The first World War broke his heart and contributed to his early death, as he felt that Germany, the land of his spiritual birth, was running amok and turning their finest thought and energy to the destruction of mankind. When it proved that his friend Münsterberg, whom he had been responsible for bringing to Harvard, was a German agent, this just about completed his heartbreak, and he died in the fall of 1916, after doing all he could to bring about war between the United States and Germany, although he had been the most pacific kind of person throughout his life.

In the last ten years of his life, he did a great deal of long and laborious work on symbolic logic, of which only a little was published because his researches were never completed. These later interests in his life and work may, to some extent, explain why his later works contain less reference to Indic philosophy than his earlier writings.

Sincerely yours,
Signed: Stephen Royce

Letter II

The special significance of this letter is that it gives Stephen Royce's version of the relations of Royce to Santayana. It also tells about Royce's ability to read Greek and Latin. Some details about his early life are also recorded here. To this letter he added this postscript: "That Papa's philosophy was essentially American can hardly be questioned with his illustrations from history and current events so frequently used." This confirms my thesis in the essay "Josiah Royce—California's Gift to Philosophy."

October 5th, 1950

Daniel S. Robinson,
Director of the School of Philosophy,
University of Southern California,
Los Angeles 7, California.

Dear Mr. Robinson:

This further note is written after having read your essay entitled "Josiah Royce—California's Gift to Philosophy."

I have to confess to a rather personal delight in the crack you take at Santayana. As I grew up in the shade of Harvard, and very much aware of what went on in the Philosophy Department, my memory goes considerably further than you would normally expect of a member of the Harvard Class of 1910.

Santayana never was appointed to a lifetime professorship in the Philosophy Department at Harvard, and left at the end of one of his 5 year terms of appointment. That he stayed as long as he did at Harvard was largely due to my father's representations in his behalf.

Professor George Herbert Palmer, in one of his late writings telling of his long experience in the Philosophy Department at Harvard, explained the reason for Santayana's not having been carried on. He said that it was always a policy in the Philosophy Department to have as wide a variety as possible of points of view and schools of thought represented in the Department. When the question arose whether Santayana was to be given a life appointment, which would have been necessitated had he been once more reappointed, their feeling was that his philosophical views did not differ sufficiently from those of others in the Department to justify his retention. In other words, it was too much agreement that was involved, rather than disagreement. This was Palmer's very gentle way of saying that Santayana lacked originality, and was the only retort I ever heard made from the Department for years of bitter remarks by Santayana about New England pundits, puritanical prejudices, etc. Santayana seems to be better known for his adverse criticisms of Boston than for any philosophical thought of his own. My father possibly brought on himself the criticism that he was an importer of German philosophy because he frequently referred to Germany as the land of his spiritual birth.

That my father was already well started in philosophical thought before he ever left Berkeley is certainly evidenced by his Baccalaureate address on "Aeschylus, Prometheus Bound." It is hard to understand how he ever wrote this at the age of approximately 20. If you do not, you should know that the entire reading involved was in the Greek. He never used a translation of any Greek or Latin text, or for that matter of any German text. One day James came to the house and asked my mother if she could loan him Josiah's Plato and Aristotle. She produced the books and James looked at them helplessly and said, "But these are in Greek!" My mother said, "Didn't these philosophers write in Greek?" James' reply was that he had never read a word of Greek in his life.

For French and Italian my father relied mainly on my mother.

You may or may not know that he entered the University of California to study mining engineering, and was a classmate of several well-known mining engineers. His omnivorous outside reading, and his speculative mind resulted in the Prometheus essay, which so impressed a group of total strangers in Berkeley and San Francisco that they put together a loan fund to send him to Germany, feeling that he was more cut out for Philosophy than for engineering.

In order to finance a summer in Boston and to get contact with scientific and philosophical men, he worked with pick and shovel and wheelbarrow grading the University grounds, earning $100.00 to finance his Boston summer. James, Palmer, and others met him at that time and were tremendously impressed.

If you are sometime traveling East and let me know I would be very happy for you to drop up here and I could tell you a great deal about his early days, including the incident where he first met James and other lifelong associates.

His assistant at the time of his death was W. F. Kernan, who shortly thereafter went into the Army in World War I, and has continued there ever since. You may possibly remember his widely publicized proposal to attack Europe from the south, which was afterwards done in an underequipped and undermanned campaign.

My father's death was much hastened by Germany running

amuck as it did in 1914. German students* at Goettingen and Leipzic in the '70s were telling my father and other American students that Germany's next campaign, which this time would be for world conquest, would be launched in 40 years. My father little realized how accurate the blueprints were.

It was my father who selected Münsterberg for Harvard and his pro-German activities were a bitter blow to my father for he could not but feel a sense of responsibility. Throughout my boyhood Münsterberg gravely puzzled his colleagues by his frequent Sunday Supplement sensational writeups on philosophy & psychology wholly foreign to his very valuable scientific work. Shortly before his death, my father told me that this was all part of the plan, and that Münsterberg had been called in to the Wilhelmstrasse and instructed to get in the limelight so that his name should be well-known when his propaganda should become necessary to the fatherland.

> With best regards,
> Sincerely yours,
> Signed: Stephen Royce

Letter III

In this letter Stephen Royce expresses his appreciation of my sending him a copy of my edition of *Royce's Logical Essays*. He refers approvingly to the biographical sketch of his father by Professor Mary W. Calkins, of Wellesley College. There is an interesting example of the method of sampling which Stephen gave to Royce's advanced seminar in logic. Again he mentions Royce's work on symbolic logic. There is an enjoyable account of Royce toiling on his logical notations on a sailboat cruise through a southeaster storm in the Massachusetts Bay area. Note that he here claims that his father "finally completed the harmonic construction."

The question Stephen Royce asked me in this letter I referred to Josiah Royce's bibliographer, my friend Professor Frank M. Oppenheim, S.J., of Xavier University, Cincinnati, Ohio. In reply he wrote in a letter dated July 27, 1966: "The quote from Stephen Royce, June 26, 1951, is facinating and tantalizing. . . . As a possible proof of accomplishment of this 'thing' to which Stephen referred, contained in one of the Roycean Logicalia Black Boxes at the Widener (Harvard University Library) are

---

* The junkers, with the carefully cultivated saber scars.

items under the following description: ROYCE MSS: BLACK
BOX LABELLED: NOTES ON LOGIC, MATHEMATICS,
AND THEORY OF KNOWLEDGE HUG 1755.5 (3rd item on
list: a 36 pp, undated autographed notebook whose description
reads: Bears name of J. G. Gustafson. First Half: essay by Gustafson; second half: mathematical notations by Royce including
memoirs on the algebra of logic—Royce interpretating Whitehead in terms of the F-relation)."

This statement of Professor Oppenheim indicates how carefully Harvard University archivists have preserved the papers
Stephen's letter says Royce left in his office.

In a letter dated December 26, 1967, Professor Oppenheim sent
me the following marginalia, written in Josiah Royce's handwriting on page 61 of his personal copy of the German edition of
Ruge's *Encylopaedia der Philosophischen Wissenshaften*, Erster
Band, *Logik*. This copy is now in the Widener Library of Harvard University under the catalogue number Phil. 5062.18.3 It
was located in the summer of 1967 by Dr. I. J. Skrupskelis, of the
University of South Carolina, and pointed out to Professor Oppenheim and it is included here with the latter's permission. The
underscoring was done by Royce.

"*Note*. By the terms of Royce's contract with Ruge, made in
1909, the German publisher has the copyright of this essay, of
which, at the date of this publication (in 1912), no English edition exists. The general idea of Logic as the "Theory of Order,"
as here sketched, has been previously suggested in various of
Royce's essays (Cf. World & Individual, Vol. II, Lectures I and
II), but is here more fully outlined than by any previous discussion of Logic by J. R. This paper is thus a programme of a future possible Logic; and *as* a programme has a place in a fairly
extensive plan. The issues discussed have, in J. R.'s opinion, an
importance that is greater than the length of the paper indicates."

For other marginalia in Josiah Royce's handwriting see my
Anthology of Modern Philosophy, pp. 502f.

June 26th, 1951

Mr. Daniel S. Robinson, Director
School of Philosophy,
University of Southern California,
Los Angeles 7, California

Dear Mr. Robinson:

I have received from the publishers a copy of your collection of logical essays for which I wish to convey my thanks. The picture you use as a frontispiece is the one we were always quite fond of in the family.

The essays are of course largely beyond the range of an engineer. Miss Calkins, in writing the Britannica article on my father, notes that he forecast much of the modern quantum theory of physics two or three decades ahead of his time. He had me tell one of his advanced seminaries in logic about the problems involved in ore sampling in which I was engaged in the summer of 1908 at the commencement of the Nevada Consolidated's mill operation. The problem there was to produce a six to ten pound sample that would have the same analysis in all of its constituents as the 1000 tons fed into the mill in 24 hours which was represented by the sample. In discussing my presentation, he pointed out that here was one of many cases in which the principle of uniformity of nature, so basic to most laboratory physics and chemistry, did not apply because here was a case in which nature refused to be uniform, and the entire process had to allow for and counteract this lack of uniformity. He then went on to point out the basic principles of what has since become known as the quantum theory.

During the first 12 years of this century, he spent a great deal of his time on symbolic logic, filling many notebooks with computations. He mentioned that the last important work on this subject had been done something like a century before by Kempe, and that he himself hoped to live long enough to carry the work on to where the mathematicians would begin to take it up. In speaking of the mathematics of symbolic logic, he stated that it is a mathematics so broad in its implications that he viewed all of our existing mathematics as constituting a special case of the algebra of logic.

He worked off and on for years on the problem of producing in the algebra of logic the equivalent of the "harmonic construction." He finally accomplished this and I believe he published it somewhere. I do not find this listed in the symbolic logic sec-

tion of your book and am wondering if you know about it, or
could look it up. The difficulty he had in his computations was
due to the fact that a long series of transformations would often
lead him back to the starting equation instead of on to the new
relations he was seeking to prove.

In September, 1909, when he was working on the harmonic
construction, I took him on a sailboat cruise in the Cape Cod-
Martha's Vineyard-Buzzards' Bay area. His notebooks went
along with him, and when it was time to go back for college he
insisted we had to go through a southeaster that wrecked quite
a few vessels along the Cape Cod shoals. He would sit in the
cockpit figuring in his notebook and when I saw a great comber
coming I would warn him and his notebook would disappear under his slicker, to emerge after the inundation had subsided. It
was just following this cruise that he finally completed the harmonic construction. The only mathematician who had been working with him on the job was E. V. Huntington of the Mathematics
Department at Harvard. I always hoped that at some time I
would have the leisure to learn this mathematics from Huntington and go on with my father's work, but this is not going to
happen.

Has anything further been done on this symbolic logic since
my father died? His computation books on the subject were all
at Emerson Hall and I found none of them in his effects
in closing the house.

My father was afraid that if he did not get far enough in this
subject, it would lie dormant for another hundred years, whereas
if it was carried on, he felt that at some time it might aid in solv-
ing some of the higher degree equations, or in working problems
involving a space of more than three dimensions.

With best regards,
Sincerely yours,
Signed: Stephen Royce

Letter IV

Why Royce's books were put out-of-print by his publishers
during World War I and II is explained in this fourth letter.
They melted down their old electroplates to obtain copper to
make new ones, writes Stephen Royce. He refers to Professor
Cotton's efforts to get the major works of Royce republished, but
to date only *The World and the Individual,* 2 vols., (Dover Publications, Inc., New York, 1959), and *The Spirit of Modern Phi-*

losophy, (George Braziller, New York, 1955), have appeared. According to a recent announcement of Henry Regnery & Co., *The Problem of Christianity,* 2 vols., is in press and will appear shortly.

August 28th, 1952

D. S. Robinson, Director
School of Philosophy
University of Southern California
University Park
Los Angeles 7, California

Dear Dr. Robinson:

Yours of April 14th has stayed on my desk while I tried to think of something I could do about it. However, I am so completely out of touch with Philosophical people that there is little I can do to push sales. I am sorry the book does not move more rapidly because I was hoping to see a revival of my father's philosophy. Macmillan have told me that in the normal course of their publishing operations, most of his books would still be available but the combined effect of World Wars I and II wiped them out. In both wars, the copper shortage resulted in publishers being told that they could not obtain new copper for electroplating if they had electroplates on hand for books that sold less than a certain small assigned numbers of copies in the past five years. Philosophy books, and especially the more technical variety, do not have a wide popular sale. The result was that in order to keep in the publishing business, they had to keep going through their less active plates and melt them up for new publications. This wiped out several of my father's books in World War I and most of the rest in World War II. Otherwise this class of book would have been and was reprinted in lots of 1000 or 2000 every few years indefinitely.

Professor Cotton of Wabash College has been trying to get a publisher for a revival analysis of my father's ethical and metaphysical writings. Macmillan are quite favorable to the project but they tell him that they can and do put out a good many books that they expect to be unprofitable but that in order to stay in business they have to hold the unpopular list to close limits. Philosophical books of the more popular style of writing, like James, survived better under these circumstances than the more technical type like my father's.

Sincerely yours,
Signed: Stephen Royce

XVII

NINE LETTERS OF WILLIAM ERNEST HOCKING

Over the years I have received many letters from Hocking, some of which are quoted, either in part or in full, above (see p. 50, p. 98, p. 114 and p. 138). From among these letters I have selected nine for inclusion here. To clarify each letter I have written a brief prefatory comment. These letters are especially informative. They also reveal Hocking's sense of humor, his generosity, and his magnanimity. I count it a high privilege to have been under his instruction and to have had him as a life-long friend. It was always a deep joy to converse with him, and a profound satisfaction to communicate with him in writing.

There are many other letters, including his correspondence with Royce, as well as personalia, in Hocking's library at Madison, New Hampshire. This library and its contents are now in possession of his son, Professor Richard Hocking. Much of the material therein is scheduled for publication later.

Letter I

This letter is acknowledgement of receipt of two reprints I I had sent Hocking from *The Personalist,* one being my lecture "Josiah Royce—California's Gift to Philosophy," and the other, an essay on Gabriel Marcel. His comments on these articles are interesting and significant. The review of the translations of Marcel's *Metaphysical Journal* and of *Man Against Mass Society,* to which Hocking evidently refers in this letter, appeared in *The Journal of Philosophy,* Vol. 50, (1953), pp. 698-702. It was written by Mr. R. D. Comming of Columbia University. It does not even mention Marcel's acknowledged obligations to Royce and Hocking. And the footnote he mentions is his own profound study of Marcel, later published in *Philosophy and Phenomenological Research,* which Professor Marvin Farber edits. (See above, p. 75).

WILLIAM ERNEST HOCKING

Alford Professor Emeritus
Harvard University

Madison
New Hampshire
June 16, 1954

My dear Robinson,

I am delighted to have these two Personalists with your fine articles in them.

I have never had any doubt that through the busy miscellany, the tumult and the shouting of the wordy semanticisms of the day, the figure of Royce would emerge in its true stature,— taking the dimensions of the California landscape! Apart from the special views which you well trace, there was the majesty of the California world that got into him. Of course, there was a native majesty in his soul which could respond to the majesty outside; the two worked together.

It is good, too, after the pathetic attempts of somebody in Columbia to review Marcel for the Journal of Philosophy, to read something about Marcel creditable to American thought. Keep an eye out for Farber's coming number; there will be a footnote to your article.

Thanks, and congratulations.
Signed:　Ernest Hocking

Letter II

Here is one of Hocking's most informative letters. It is in response to my letter informing him of the organization of The Foundation for the Promotion of Idealistic Philosophy in America. This Foundation subsidized the publication of Marcel's *Royce's Metaphysics,* and some other philosophical activities, but it ceased to function when its sponsor withdrew his financial support. Hocking explains why idealism has had a bad press and has fallen into disrepute. His discussion of what to do about this is especially thought-provoking. He suggests that someone must "write that paragraph in which the meaning of idealism is so transparent and radiant that it will compel its own attention and conviction." His comment on Rousseau is penetrating. His rejection of any participation in the work of the Foundation is firmly stated. Note well his statement: "The trail of the serpent is over all organization."

WILLIAM ERNEST HOCKING

Alford Professor Emeritus
Harvard University

Madison
New Hampshire
May 11, 1954

My dear Robinson,

Like you, I have for a long time been concerned over what we
might call the "bad press" which idealism has been suffering
under. In spite of the irrelevance of the notion of "fashion" to
the world of ideas, there is no doubt that in this country, and to
some extent in Europe, there has ruled an anti-idealistic fashion.
And strangely enough in a field where care in the use of terms
should rule, this current has been opposed less to idealism than
to subjectivism with which it is too easy to identify idealism.
In your statement, you have put this matter just right, by defining idealism as a view of "being," a metaphysic, not an epistemological vestibule. When Reinhold Niebuhr or John Wild
denounces idealism, or when Gabriel Marcel overcomes the idealism of Hegel and moves somewhat unawares in the direction of
Kierkegaard, they are not opposing the thesis that ideas are
real, but the thesis that the real consists of (our) ideas pure and
simple. It is a matter of great importance to get idealism as a
metaphysic presented as it is, and not as those who seek the air
of novelty by an illicit contrast would like to present it. (I am
not accusing Marcel of this; he is a serious writer, and Farber
is publishing—I think in June—a full-length review of his work,
which I hope will straighten out a few strands in the recent history of ideas.)

Now what to do about this is a hard question.

My feeling is that what you have been doing is extremely effective, and exactly to the point. When you got Royce's essays in
logic between covers, you did it at precisely the right time; there
has been a widespread—and highly indefinite—feeling that
Royce has been neglected, and that here we have a thinker of the
first rank who deserves a second and third and fourth look. (And
perhaps I have already written you about Marcel's small book,
1945, La métaphysique de Royce, which is a capital summari-
zation and should be translated.) And your own writings, and
your historical notes, as in Farber's book on French-and-Ameri-
can thought, are doing great service in the essential task, of

making clear what idealism means *in terms of experience in all its phases.*

When we do more than this, and set up an organization to promote idealism, we run a risk. We do things that need to be done, but we do them by an identifiable and timable stroke of will of which, if we succeed, it could be said that "Idealism is coming up again, because X, Y, and Z are giving it a boost." The opposite policy, that of laissez faire, seems relatively passive and stupid, and if we do nothing more it is exactly that. But there is no danger, my dear Robinson, that you will ever be either passive or stupid or both! You will be working to the end of your days,—and I am giving myself to the same effort so far as circumstances permit—to write *that paragraph* in which the meaning of idealism is so transparent and radiant that it will compel its own attention and conviction, and spread through the whole network of human mentality. That may take a hundred years, but what does that matter?

Rousseau made a wonderful blunder. He opened his Social Contract with a sentence that struck every reader immediately, between the eyes, and gave him an unforgettable impression that Rousseau *did not intend!* He said "Man is born free, and everywhere he is in chains." And thousands of readers have said, "How true, let us cast off the chains." But what Rousseau meant, and proceeded to say, was that this paradoxical situation is one he proposes to explain and in some measure to justify! There is a civil liberty that is better than natural liberty; that is his thesis and an anarchistic revolution is precisely its denial. Yet that blazing opening line has stirred how many a chain-destroying impulse!

The problem of idealism's repute in the world is, so far as I can grasp it, to write a line equally blazing, but one which cannot be misunderstood! Man is born in the freedom and unity of the Spirit, but everywhere he is in the chains of bodily separation: will not do me as it is.

I am stupid about organizations. I belong to the church, because I believe in belonging, and in the corporate living and action of souls inspired by a common tradition and a common faith. But I belong to the Congregationalists, who are the most anti-organizational of all organized bodies, and who suffer from the consequences of their own logic, of being incapable of effective corporate action. You may be able to resolve that paradox; I have to live in its snags and trust in God for the outcome. When

I was studying missions in the Orient,—and missions are an attempt to do something positive through organizations,—I wrote a line which my commission refused to print: "The trail of the serpent—I wrote—is over all organization,"—I was thinking of the vested interests that clutter the intricate architecture of the church. The Commission was entirely right in cutting that sentence out, it was a merely Congregationalist sentence! But that is the way I am.

And so, whatever you propose to do by way of a Foundation, I will say to it, God bless you. But I shall be of no help in its construction; here I belong to the passive *and* stupid class.

Yours "in the unity of the Spirit"
    and with enduring affection,

Signed: Ernest Hocking

Letter III

I wrote Hocking about our plans to publish a translation of Marcel's *Royce's Metaphysics,* and this letter is his reply. Again he refers to his own article: "Marcel and the Ground Issues of Metaphysics." He also mentions professor Ducasse's visit with Marcel in Paris, and Dr. Boctor. The latter did a dissertation on Hocking's metaphysical outlook. He taught in Cairo.

WILLIAM ERNEST HOCKING

Alford Professor Emeritus
Harvard University

Madison
New Hampshire
July 11, 1954

My dear Robinson,
    Yours of July 1 brings me much welcome news.
    I am especially glad to hear of the prospect of a translation of Marcel's Royce. Farber has already sent Marcel a copy of the Marcel article in his Journal; and I shall write him when the reprints come along, sending him one of them. I shall take the occasion to mention the translation, and to forward your suggestion of a preface or introduction.
    He has probably had some wind of the article through Boctor and Ducasse. Ducasse has seen him, this Spring, at some conference of parapsychologists in France. And Boctor, a young chap who has just taken his Doctor of Letters under Jean Wahl, with

a thesis on my metaphysical outlook, has had a conference or two with Marcel. My own correspondence with Marcel came to an end in the early twenties, when Marcel got wrapped up in the presentation of one of his plays, Le Coeur des Autres. But I have some hope he will want to say something in reply.

If you and Mrs. Robinson come as near as West Virginia this coming year, perhaps you will be able to swing around this way. It would be a pleasure to see you.

Sincerely,
Signed: Ernest Hocking

P.S. Boctor, who is teaching philosophy in Cairo, will have an article, probably in the November number, of *The Review of Religion,* Columbia, on "Outline-sketch of a Philosophy of Joy," as a counterpart to the prevalent existentialist emphasis on *angoisse.*

Letter IV

In this letter Hocking indicates his continued serious interest in helping with the translation of Marcel's book. This is evidence of his generosity.

WILLIAM ERNEST HOCKING

Alford Professor Emeritus
Harvard University

Madison
New Hampshire
October 2, 1954

My dear Robinson,

Looking back on our recent correspondence, I find in your letter of August 12 the question "Would you be willing to read the translation before we forward it to Marcel?" I hadn't realized until seeing that sentence again that you may be waiting for some word from me regarding the translation.

I have sampled it, and find it good.

There are points to cavil at here and there, and some slips such as are likely to come into any translation; but the meaning is given with fidelity, and with a good flow of English, secured by a wise freedom from precise adherence to the French sentence-structure. There are occasional obscurities in Marcel's text, but it is to me a constant surprise, considering how elusive some of

Marcel's later writings are, to see how tangible and direct this discussion of Royce is.

Now my question is, how much careful scrutiny of the whole translation do you want me to make? I note that the schedule is a little behind what you anticipated, and it might be better not to wait for the work of a fine-tooth comb. Marcel would himself be disposed, I believe, to examine it for its major qualities. However, I want to do what you would like me to do; this is an important piece, and the other pressures on me at the moment shall not interfere any more than I can help.

I shall put on another sheet notes of points in the translation which I would query, in the Introduction only, mentioning simply that no two translators will agree on every rendering. And then, I await your further instructions, realizing that the opening of every college-term is a time of intense busyness, especially in a new corner of the world, way up in the squeeze of West Virginia, where you have to watch your balance to keep from falling on one side into Penna and on the other into Ohio, or *the* Ohio.

All good wishes,
Sincerely,
Signed: Ernest Hocking

Letter V

This letter was handwritten at the Massachusetts General Hospital where Hocking was convalescing from a serious knee operation. He describes his experience of being in a hospital. Then he expresses his appreciation of our note of sympathy to him over the death of his wife, Agnes Hocking. He tells about her funeral services. In this letter he enclosed the handwritten statement: "On the Centenary Year of Royce's Birth," which is reproduced above (see pp. 82f).

Phillips House
Massachusetts General Hospital
265 Charles Street
Boston, Massachusetts

July 25, 1955

My dear Robinson,

Your kind letter of the 20th with its words of sympathy on the death of Agnes Hocking, reaches me this morning, where I am taking an enforced vacation owing to a broken knee requiring an operation—the first time I have enjoyed this rather common human experience. All has gone well & I shall soon be back at the farm, with all the children, but with rather hampered freedom of movement for a few weeks.

This will explain a certain delay—your letter had to be forwarded—in replying to your request for a word addressed to the centenary meeting, which I am glad to offer. I heard Loewenberg's speech at B.U. (Boston University), and it is a good one. You will make allowance for the circumstance of this letter, and if my words do not seem to rise to the occasion, please feel free to discard them. I am still hoping that Harvard may come through with something, perhaps in the anniversary month—November, wasn't it?

I am glad that the fragment of Agnes Hocking's letter reached you and your wife prior to her death. We had a service for her at Madison, among neighbors, another at Mount Auburn, and it was a delight to know how many remembered and cared about her. I am not sure you remember Woodworth, organist, successor to "Doc" Davison, with choir and glee-club. "Woody" we call him—well, "Woody" played on that occasion, beginning with her favorite chorale "Deck thyself, my soul, with gladness." It was an occasion of thanksgiving for a noble life.

With warm regards,
Signed: Ernest Hocking

Letter VI

This letter was also written in longhand from the hospital. Hocking expresses his delight over the information that Henry Regnery and Company had contracted to publish Marcel's *Royce's Metaphysics*. He agreed to write an Introduction to the book.

Massachusetts General Hospital

Phillips House
265 Charles Street
Boston, Massachusetts.

My dear Robinson:
Yours of the 12th reaches me here. I hope to be a free man in a few days.

I am delighted that Regnery will publish the translation of Marcel's Royce. I didn't get a chance to look it through in detail —there were points to correct in the early pages, & someone should really check the whole thing. I simply endorsed the translation as, on the whole, good, and have kept after Regnery on its behalf. I take it that the translators will not be averse to suggestions of a minor sort, if we find details that need revision?

In any case, I shall be glad to do something by way of an Introduction—though I am not up to anything really adequate at present. I am due to write a segment of a three-some on Royce for the December meeting—to be presented by Smith and Richard Hocking as the mainstays of the triad. Perhaps something of this would fit into the scheme of the Introduction.

I was also asked by the Harvard Department to give a Centenary Lecture on Royce, but have had to decline on the score that I have no voice left for public speaking. I did agree to say a few words about how Royce happened to come to Harvard as a story every Harvard man should know. No date is set for this event as yet.

I shall look forward to your "Crucial Issues."

With thanks and greetings
Yours sincerely
Signed: Ernest Hocking

Letter VII

This letter tells of his admiration for Lutoslawski, and of his arrangements with Gabriel Marcel to write a special Foreword for the English edition of *Royce's Metaphysics.*

WILLIAM ERNEST HOCKING

Alford Professor Emeritus
Harvard University

Madison
New Hampshire
July 30, 1956

My dear Robinson,

Your letter of the 28th reaches me just now, I being the mailboy for today. All the able-bodied are haying, and I am the loafer, fit to drive a car to the P.O. for outgoing and incoming mail. We had a pleasant visit from Mollenhauer a few weeks back, on the theme of Lutoslawski, an object of mutual admiration, who visited us in Berkeley in 1907-8, and with whom I corresponded up to 1949. I note the element of urgency in the matter of Foreword for the Royce translation, and shall try to get this to you by return of post.

I made the suggestion to Regnery some time back that he might raise the question with Marcel as to a Foreword. He thought well of the idea, wrote Marcel; and to this letter Marcel responded in a letter to me, in substance as follows: He would be unable to follow the suggestion that he tell how he became interested in Royce's work; he could not recall the story but could sketch his present attitude to Royce. I immediately replied that this would be the ideal thing, adding a speculation of my own as to how, via Bradley's argument from the infinite regress, Marcel was led to Royce from Bradley, and remarked that he might be moved to correct my mythology, though it was obviously out of the question to resurrect the forgotten details.

Both Regnery and I have been waiting a response to this letter but so far in vain; and perhaps Marcel means silence to mean that the divine spark has not yet entered. I agreed to write a brief note of introduction, in the absence of something better; and shall now begin to plan for a note of this sort, though I am frightfully busy and behind on present engagements with Harpers and Scribners,— the latter firm reissuing TYPES, after 25 years, calling for much rewriting.

Regards and good wishes,
Signed: Ernest Hocking

Letter VIII

In this letter Hocking asks whether I can supply him with biographical information about Royce requested by Professor André A. Devaux, whose excellent Royce Bibliography is listed under *Bibliographies* below. He explains that he lost track of Royce's two sons, whose names were Stephen and Edward, twenty years ago, and he adds that he never knew George Buchanan Coale to whom Royce dedicated *The Religious Aspect of Philosophy.*

WILLIAM ERNEST HOCKING

Alford Professor Emeritus
Harvard University

Madison
New Hampshire
March 1, 1960

My dear Robinson,

You have doubtless been hearing from Professor André A.

Devaux, who is working on Royce—doing what he calls "une étude d'ensemble." He has sent me a number of questions, some of which I can't answer; and perhaps you have some helpful trails.

Like everybody working on Royce, he wants more biography, a theme which Royce deliberately kept in scant supply; and in that interest asks whether any of Royce's descendants are accessible. Two sons were living, some twenty years ago; but I have wholly lost track of them. Have you any clues?

He also asks about the person to whom Royce dedicated "The Religious Aspect of Philosophy." George Buchanan Coale. I never knew. (I have had some correspondence with Dover Publications, who are disposed to reprint this work.)

It is a joy to see Royce coming into his own.

Cordial greetings and warmest regards,
Signed: Ernest Hocking

Letter IX

This is the last letter I received from Hocking. It is quoted in part above (see p. 98). I had sent him the essay "Hocking's Contribution to Idealistic Metaphysics," and I had requested him to confirm some biographical references in it. In this letter he answered my question about D. C. Macintosh's criticism of his *Meaning of God in Human Experience.* He also makes effective use of a passage from Whitehead, and mentions his work on his Gifford Lectures, and his collaboration with the physicist, Frederick Werner, on atomic physics. I have discussed these points in the *In Memoriam Essay* above (see pp. 79ff).

WILLIAM ERNEST HOCKING

Alford Professor Emeritus
Harvard University

Madison
New Hampshire
September 22, 1964

Professor Daniel S. Robinson,
3640 Homeland Drive
Los Angeles 8, California

My dear Robinson:

I am very much in your debt for this article of yours for Rouner's kindly and taxing enterprise—taxing to himself, and to numerous others of my dearest colleagues and friends.

I should have sent it on its return journey yesterday were it not for the fact that I wanted to make my own notes from your pages—data that I had lost track of, and which I feel an increasing need of being able to recover, and can now re-read owing to that kind of masterly enquiry and discussion which is your gift. (Your Story of Scottish Philosophy is a continuing delight.)

There is nothing I would want to alter in these pages. I have pencilled a few trifles of typing, such as Gilman's Bibliography (not Biography) page 5, and on page 6 the title of the Marcel article, "the Ground Issues . . ."

Particularly grateful to you for your recovery of the Macintosh criticism: all that you say about that is helpful and just. The spatial language of my report in Meaning of God is both inadequate and misleading. Yet it is hard to find an equivalent for the metaphorical "within." Whitehead finds the same difficulty in that important passage in which he reverses his denial that the world can be "in the mind" (Nature and Life, page 40). "Thus, in a sense, the experienced world is one complex factor in the composition of many factors constituting the essence of the soul. We can phrase this shortly by saying that in one sense the world is in the soul." He refers later on the page to "this baffling antithetical relation" whereby I am in the room and in another sense the room is in me!

Just now I am engaged in two rather exacting undertakings, putting the Gifford Lectures into order, and coming to terms with the newer developments of atomic physics. There is at Xavier University in Cincinnati a remarkable young physicist, Frederick Werner, who has been close to Niels Bohr both here and in Copenhagen, and who is convinced that the paradox of "Complementarity" needs a metaphysical answer, with some reference to the "union of opposites." He is making some use of my view of the Self as a "field of fields"; and so we get together occasionally for deep plotting to introduce metaphysics into physics without creating a communist revolution in cosmology.

But this is another story, except that it constitutes another motive for not wanting to leave the scene until these fascinating chores are finished.

With grateful regards,
Always yours,
Signed: Ernest Hocking

The above letter is typed. Then, after signing it, he added in his own handwriting the following request and the little rhyme or doggerel.

If at any time you are typing this, would you put in an extra carbon and let me have it for reference?

"Put on the pot
Said Greedy Sot
We'll sup before we go."

BIBLIOGRAPHIES

Some Roycean Bibliographies (arranged chronologically)

RAND, Benjamin. "A Bibliography of the Writings of Josiah Royce," *Philosophical Review*, XXV, No. 3 (May, 1916), 515-22.

LOEWENBERG, J. "A Bibliography of the Unpublished Writings of Josiah Royce," *Philosophical Review*, XXVI (1917), 578-82.

SMITH, John E. "Bibliography," *Royce's Social Infinite* (New York: Liberal Arts Press, 1950), pp. 171-73.

COTTON, J. Harry. "Selected Bibliography," *Royce on the Human Self* (Cambridge: Harvard University Press, 1954), pp. 305-11.

HERNANDEZ, Victoria, and Others (Boyd Cruise and Frank M. Oppenheim, S.J.). *Index to the Josiah Royce Papers.* Unpublished Guide to the Roycean MSS Folios (98 vols.) and Boxes (14), reserved at the Widener Library Archives, Harvard University. Completed in 1958.

HUMBACH, Karl-Theo. "Bibliographie der Schriften von und über Royce," *Das Verhältnis von Einzelperson und Gemeinschaft nach Josiah Royce* (Heidelberg: Carl Winter Universitätsverlag, 1962), Anhang II, pp. 181-201.

FUSS, Peter. "Bibliography," *The Moral Philosophy of Josiah Royce* (Cambrige: Harvard University Press, 1965), pp. 265-68.

OPPENHEIM, Frank M. "A Critical Annotated Bibliography of the Published Works of Josiah Royce," *The Modern Schoolman*, St. Louis, Vol. XLI, 1964, pp. 339-65. Revised edition in *Revue* etc. pp. 138-158, cited in the next item.

DEVAUX, André A. "Bibliographie des traductions d'ouvrages de Royce et des etudes sur l'oeuvre de Royce," *Revue Internationale de Philosophie,* Numbro 79-80, Facicule 1-2, pp. 159-82.

For Biographies of Josiah Royce, see:

(1) *Encyclopedia Britannica,* 1961 ed. By Mary W. Calkins and William E. Hocking.

(2) *Encyclopedia of the Social Sciences,* (1934), by William E. Hocking.

(3) *Dictionary of American Biography,* 1958, by Ralph Barton Perry.

(4) *The Encyclopedia of Philosophy,* 1967, by John E. Smith.

Bibliographies of William Ernest Hocking

GILMAN, RICHARD C. "The Bibliography of William Ernest Hocking from 1898 to 1951," Colby College, Waterville, Maine, 1951.

GILMAN, RICHARD C. "The Bibliography of William Ernest Hocking from 1898 to 1964," From *Philosophy, Religion, and the Coming World Civilization. Essays in Honor of William Ernest Hocking,* Edited by Leroy S. Rouner, (The Hague, Martinus Nijhoff, 1966), Pp. 464-504. Fully annotated. This book also contains Professor Rouner's "The Making of a Philosopher: Ernest Hocking's Early Years." See also President Richard C. Gilman's brief biography in *The Encyclopedia of Philosophy,* 1967.

INDEX

A

Absolute, 32, 71, 65f., 92f., XII
Absolute pragmatism, 60f., 71
Aeschylus, 148, 151
Alcalde, 22
Algebra of logic, 53f.
Allinson, B. D., 11, 33f.
American Journal of Mathematics, 143
Anaximander, 36
Anselm, St., 94
Aquinas, St. T., 39, 99
Aristotle, 26, 37, 57f., 99, 151
Aristotelian Society, 139
Atomic bombs, 83, 102
Axioms, 46, 60f.

B

Baldwin, M., 35ff., 45, 57
Being, 39, 93
Bergson, H., 103
Berkeley, G., 25
Bibliography, 63, 85, 171f.
Boctor, Dr., 161f.
Bohr, N., 84, 168
Bosanquet, B., 93, 125
Bowne, B. P., 66, 75
Bradley, F. H., 92f., 166
Brightman, E. S., 121, 139
Broad, C. D., 50, 55
Browning, R., 47
Bruno, G., 25, 99
Buddha, 116

C

California, I., 65, 79
Calkins, M. W., 152, 154
Carr, H. W., 139
Categories, 42
Chatterji, J. C., 145
Clark University, 137, 138
Coale, G. B., 166f.
Cohen, M. R., 59, 62
Coherence theory of truth, 61
Columbia University, 150, 157
Comming, R. D., 157
Commotive process, 101
Comte, A., 65
Conscience, 67, 72

Contradiction, 53, 56
Contrite consciousness, 135
Correspondence theory of truth, 60
Costello, H. T., 10, 45ff., 62f.
Cotton, H., 143, 155, 156
Cultural pluralism, 108

D

Darwin, C., 65
Democracy, 112, 118
Denazification, 112
Descartes, R., 116
Devaux, A. A., 166f.
Devaux, P., 10, 13
Dewey, J., 20, 71, 85
Dialectical method, 42f., 57f., 96f., 101
Distinctions, 39f.
Division of labor, 27f.
Double translation theory, 73
Ducasse, C. J., 63, 161

E

Eaton, R. M., 63
Education, Experiment in, X, XI
Edwards, J., 31
Emerson, R. W., 31, 120, 145
Encyclopedia Britannica, 143
Engels, F., 12
Eucken, R., 37
Existentialism, 116f.
Experience, 23f., 42, 68
Extracts from "A Vocabulary," 137f.

F

Facsimiles, 82f., 130f.
Farber, M., 10, 81, 157f., 161
Faust, 54f.
Feeling as cognitive, 89
Fichte, J. G., 20, 92, 99, 109, 120
Fisch, M., 129
Frankfurter, F., 107

G

Geometry, 51
Gerig, John L., 145
Germany, X, XI
Gifford Lectures, 65, 74, 84, 118, 126, 168

173